Managing Conflict

Managing Conflict
The Key to Making
Your Organization Work

Dean Tjosvold
Simon Fraser University

Team Media
1555 118th Lane NW
Minneapolis, Minnesota 55433

ISBN 0-9621542-0-2

Library of Congress Card Catalog Number: 88-040531

Printed in the United States of America

89 90 91 6 5 4 3 2

This book is dedicated to those leaders
who value, not fear, our diversity.

Table of Contents

Table of Contents

Table of Contents

Preface

Since Fredrick Taylor, managers have worked to make their organizations efficient by removing conflict. Yet we have good reasons to challenge the wisdom of avoiding conflict.

Conflict reaches into every part of work and management. Employees can avoid and hide from conflict, but they cannot escape it.

People in the workplace even experience conflict over how to manage conflict. Most believe that they must maintain harmony; others, that they should yell and shout. People are often confused about whether they can deal directly with frustrations and problems. They are unsure whether another's silence means support for their position or a cladestine attempt to sabotage them.

The good news is that many studies show that **conflict, when well-handled, is a powerful, constructive force that breathes life and energy into the workplace.** A shared vision and strong culture, participation, labor-management cooperation, synergy and integration, project teams, task forces, and other management innovations all become empty slogans without positive conflict.

Conflict can be managed for productive ends. Research strongly supports this conclusion. (See the Reference Note at the end of the book for reviews of the literature.) Yet, perhaps understandably, for some long-held beliefs die slowly, managers resist taking a more favorable, opportunistic view toward conflict.

People often find the idea of managing conflict abstract and elusive. But conflict is a very earthy issue. For this reason, I have chosen to write this book in a narrative, more real-like fashion. **The story in Managing Conflict allows the reader to see conflict at work.** Concise explanations use the story to explore major ideas about conflict in organizations.

Reading this book can put you and your colleagues on the same wavelength. You can have a shared understanding that conflict revitalizes teamwork and friendship. You can begin to develop a shared confidence that by dealing with conflict openly and skillfully you can make it work for you and your company. I expect you to find something useful in this book; I hope you pass it around.

Acknowledgements

This book joins research and practice. I want to thank the many researchers who have contributed to the theories and evidence that created the book's framework. I also gratefully acknowledge the ideas, cases, and questions many managers have shared with me that refined and filled out that framework and documented how it could be applied in many work settings. I have learned a great deal from these discussions and controversies.

Bill Swanson confidently proposed the narrative approach to telling the story of conflict in organizations. Mary and Margaret Tjosvold demonstrated many ways to make conflict positive. Bruce Katz carefully edited the book and made helpful suggestions. Bob Birtch designed the cover and Patricia Hort professionally prepared the manuscript. I thank the nice people at Team Media for their enthusiasm in publishing an innovative management book. Jenny Tjosvold helped mold the presentation, and with our sons and daughter, provided a supportive, conflict-positive environment for working and living.

SECTION I
CONFLICT IN ORGANIZATIONS

Chapter 1
Introduction

"You've come for the whole show, I hope," Joe Shara, Chief Executive Officer of Heart Technologies, Inc., said to Brian Quillan. Joe's greeting conveyed both warmth and deference to the man whose electronic heart pacers had been critical to Heart Tech's growth and success in its first nine years.

Joe had met Brian eleven years ago at a medical technologies conference in New Orleans. He had been so impressed with Brian's work and ideas that he started Heart Tech in Brian's hometown, Minneapolis. Joe then built the organization around Brian's inventions.

"No, I hadn't planned on staying," Brian replied. "I need to take off after my presentation and get back to work. I'll let you manage the company. You're good at it."

Joe gently pressed the point. "It would be good to have you there. These management meetings are very informative. Everyone gets a chance to tell what they're doing and catch up on what's happening with the company as a whole. Sometimes we even get around to solving a problem. We've got some good people working for us, Brian. I wish you'd get to know them better."

"Well, maybe I could stay a little longer," Brian said, "but you know how obsessed I am with my projects. Besides, we're meeting a researcher from the University who might be able to help us on the lithium-powdered pacer."

"Of course," said Joe. He didn't want to push Brian. Yet he wanted Brian to take the management meetings and team more seriously. "It's hard to believe that we'll be celebrating our tenth anniversary," he said, changing the subject. "We've had our ups and downs, but we've come a long way, haven't we? You don't have to work in a garage any longer!"

"We've changed a lot," Brian mused. "I sort of miss the old days. We were so energetic and committed—and so innocent. Things seem so much more complicated now."

"Things like management meetings!" Joe said, grinning. "Seriously, I'm very pleased with the management team we're developing. People feel better informed and have a broader view of the company since we began meeting every other week. There seems to be a greater sense that we're all in this together, you know? At least, we're moving in that direction. It would be a great achievement for us."

"We had a lot of that team feeling when we began," Brian said. "Now we're so big. It would be great to get the team feeling back. But please, let's not have meeting after meeting!"

Joe knew that many people at Heart Tech were skeptical of meetings, but he hoped the management team would be different. There was no crises, at least not yet. But Joe knew that their products were nearing the end of their cycle, and they needed to create new competitive advantages, or face a gloomy future. He wanted neither complancy nor panic, but for the people at Heart Tech to feel a greater urgency to take control of their future.

"The management meetings, I think, can help us feel more like a team and become more innovative," Joe said. "Besides, they give me a chance to keep reminding everyone that if we're going to get back on the growth track and keep the competition at bay, we just can't keep doing the same old thing. We must get smarter. This business is such a challenge today. We need smart marketing, reliable and efficient production and, of course, outstanding products. That's why we need a team approach."

"It ain't easy running a business today," Brian said.

"Hey, but it's fun!" Joe replied. "Look, it's 3 o'clock. Let's head down to the meeting."

As the two of them walked toward the conference room, Joe found himself feeling somewhat nervous. The meetings were very important to him. Heart Tech was at a critical juncture in its history. It had good people working for it, and its products were first rate. But the world had gotten much more complicated. There was, for one thing, a lot more competition now than before. This, together with the incredible advances made in the technology, made it imperative that his people work together smoothly and efficiently. They had to pool their considerable talents to keep ahead of the conglomerates that were so hungrily eyeing the medical technologies market. But he was becoming increasingly aware of internal problems at Heart Tech. There seemed to be a growing amount of conflict and disunity among his senior staff. He didn't doubt for a moment their commitment to Heart Tech—he knew them all well enough for that not to be an issue—but he was troubled by the conflict that seemed to drain so much of their energy and slow them down.

Barbara Newton, Vice President Finance, Les McKeon, VP-Marketing, and Gary Eckberg, VP-Human Resources, were already in the conference room when Joe and Brian entered. After exchanging greetings, Joe said, "While we wait for Al, I have an announcement. We have evidence that even the young get old. Today is Les's birthday!" Everyone applauded and congratulated Les. It was the first birthday he had celebrated at Heart Tech.

Then Al Gustafson, VP-Production, walked in, and Joe began the meeting.

"As you're all aware," he began, "We're not the only ones who know there's a market for heart pacers. In today's competitive market, there's no substitute for being smart. That's why these meetings are important. They give us a chance to focus on our problems, and turn problems into opportunities. They also allow us to work more like a team."

Joe smiled and continued. "My goal for our tenth anniversary is a 'Team at Ten.' "

Gary laughed. "Perhaps we first should have tea for two before we have a team for ten," he joked.

Les added: "Joe's a natural marketer—we need someone like you in our department."

Joe replied, "But then one of you would have to take my job, and none of you would want to do that!" Everyone laughed.

"We do have a reason for being here, and perhaps we'd best get back to it," Joe continued. "In addition to the usual reports from the various departments, Brian will let us know what's happening in research and development."

Brian briefly described modifications and products undergoing tests or out for government-approval. Looking up from his notes now and then to see how Joe and the others were taking in what he was saying, he explained that the approval process was getting more complicated and time-consuming. He talked enthusiastically about projects now getting under way in the lab. Although his talk was long and often technical, his colleagues listened attentively, and, when finished, asked polite questions.

Then Brian thanked everyone for listening, excused himself, and was gone.

Joe called for the next report. "Barbara, could you let us know what is happening in finance."

Barbara, though only 37, exuded credibility. Her academic credentials and executive experience with a New York bank had satisfied creditors that the company would exercise financial discipline to offset its freewheeling image. She was well prepared for her presentation. "Our overall financial profile is still stable," she began. She explained that, compared to the same quarter last year, production costs had levelled off, development costs were rising fast but were not yet a major burden, sales revenues were up modestly, and investments were performing well. She observed that the company might wish to find another bank because NorthBank may be losing interest in high tech companies. "Richard, the new contracts administrator, is getting on board nicely," she concluded. "Overall, our operation seems to be running quite smoothly. Does anyone have questions?"

Gary asked for more information on NorthBank, then Al asked questions to clarify his understanding of the financial data. Les, meanwhile, quietly sat thinking about something that had been troubling him for some time. He wasn't sure that this was the right time to bring it up-he wasn't at all sure how Joe would respond-but it was important. Taking a deep breath, he said, "I don't know about the other groups, but I think we might have a problem with Richard. Some of my sales reps raise their eyebrows and start to grumble when even his name is mentioned. They say he's tough and difficult to work with. He tells them they can't sell to several hospitals and clinics because they haven't proved they have the expertise to use our products. We lost those sales, and those doctors—not to mention our sales reps—were very unhappy."

"Richard is a bit rough around the edges," said Barbara quickly. "But he's very committed to his job and wants to do it right. We can't sell to people who do not have the know-how to use our products correctly. We leave ourselves open to lawsuits; the company could go bankrupt quickly. I'm sure he'll work out."

"I agree it's a good idea to have Richard check on whether customers have the expertise to use our product, but have we really thought through Richard's role?" Les wondered.

"Richard needs to be given a chance," Barbara insisted. "I'll keep an eye on him." Suddenly she smiled. "Don't worry, Les. You shouldn't have to grow older on your birthday!" The others in the room chuckled; they admired Barbara's ability to handle herself in a meeting.

Les quickly concluded that his persistence would only irritate Barbara and make him look like a trouble-maker. Besides, a verbal fist fight with someone as quick-tongued as Barbara would not show himself at his best. Instead, he smiled faintly, lowered his eyes, and kept quiet. He was, however, still upset, though it was not until after the meeting that he figured out why. Not only had his concern about Richard been peremptorily dismissed, but he was also being asked to laugh off what struck him as a legitimate concern, one that had an impact on everyone in the room.

Joe was sympathetic, but unsure about how he could best help Les. He didn't want to address what had happened without giving the matter some thought first. Finally, he asked, "Any other questions? If not, let's move on to Les's report."

Quickly Les told himself, Speaking up about Richard at least got my adrenaline flowing, but now I must appear composed and confident. He then began clearly, but more quickly than usual:

"My special mandate since I arrived here nine months ago was to develop new markets. Improving sales and developing business are very important to our goal of being the best heart-pacer company in the country. We are not as far as I would like to be in devising new marketing strategies, but we are mulling over several options. We think that Eastern Europe and Russia might be lucrative markets. They wouldn't be large, but we could charge what we wanted." He went on to list other marketing issues.

"Might I make a suggestion?" Al interrupted. Al was usually quiet at the meetings; he accepted the need to share information, but he seldom questioned the other managers. He would, however, put in a good word for his pet ideas when he saw the opportunity. "I don't think we give people enough reason to go that extra step in taking advantage of new market opportunities," he said. "It seems to me that creating incentives and having the sales people compete for them would be very useful. That would give them reason to go all out. Big rewards for big success."

Already agitated by his brief clash with Barbara, Les was quick to react. "Al, our sales people already work on a commission. I don't think that bigger and better commissions are the answer."

"But have you really tried?" Al countered. "It's just common sense that people will go all out when they're adequately rewarded. What we need are go-getters, and I think incentives can motivate people. We're going to try to do that in production, and it seems such a natural for marketing."

"I just don't think that kind of incentive system will help much," Les replied. "Our sales people are already motivated. It seems to me that incentives would only add a new level of competition, set my people against each other. What happens when one gets so much more money than another?"

"That would be great." Al exclaimed. "That would show everyone what we want!"

Les and Al went back and forth with quick, sharp exchanges. The others listened carefully, but were reluctant to break into the debate. Finally Joe interrupted. "What do other people feel about incentives and marketing?"

"The people I've talked with say incentive plans don't work the way they're supposed to," said Barbara. "People get upset because they think the plan isn't fair. People won't help each other unless they have a reason to do so, and competing for incentives takes away that reason."

"Incentives plans work," Gary put in. "At least they can work as well as most management schemes."

As they listened to Barbara and Gary going back and forth, both Les and Al began to think about incentive programs a little differently. Without their being aware of it, the discussion had turned from proving who was right or wrong to understanding incentives and what role they may have in marketing.

After everyone had a chance to talk, Joe said: "We won't be able to settle all the pros and cons of incentive plans today. If we do choose to use incentives at some point, we must carry out the program thoughtfully. But I think the issue is much larger than incentive plans. We really need to take some time and do some thinking and research, particularly in the context of marketing. We've got to make long-term plans. I think it's unrealistic to expect Les and his group to develop marketing plans alone. Marketing strategy involves the whole company."

"Developing marketing plans is complicated," Les said, glad that Joe had stepped in. "I like the idea of getting everyone involved. Perhaps the marketing group could get together and make preliminary proposals, think about what kind of input we need from other departments."

"Sounds good. I like that," Joe said. "Somewhere down the line the rest of us can get involved. Let's all give it some thought, OK?"

The others agreed that they should all discuss marketing with their people.

Then Al made his presentation. In his clear, precise style, he spoke of his efforts to reduce costs, his plans for an incentive system, and his recent discussions with suppliers about costs, quality, and deliveries.

Al's report concluded without interruptions or questions. The meeting was running long, and the others were getting restless.

Gary made his presentation short and breezy. "I know you're all dying to hear my report—you all probably need heart pacers to keep going." Gary's weary colleagues appreciated his sense of humor. No one had any questions.

"Other business?" Joe asked. "None? Well, thank you all for coming. Sometimes it's hard to say what tangible good has come out of our meetings, but I hope you all feel more in touch with what's going on at Heart Tech."

Barbara was reassuring. "I certainly feel much better informed. It helps communication."

"I'm glad to hear that," Joe said. "Now I hope everyone can make it for the big volleyball game."

The management team, together with some 15 other employees, gathered at the gym the company rented from a nearby church. The managers felt somewhat pressured to attend, but they and the other employees looked forward to the camaraderie and exercise. For a while they had maintained the same teams from game to game, but the competition soon became too serious. Now they chose up new sides each time. The losers had to buy the first round of beer, but everyone understood that the goal was to have fun, not simply win games. The group had developed rituals; an afternoon did not go by without a rendition of "You Gotta Have Heart." This particular afternoon they added words for Les's birthday.

After the game, they stopped by Pete's Pub for beer. Joe found himself sitting next to Les and asked the question that was nagging him. "As the newest member of the team, what do you think of our management meetings?"

Les looked unsurely at his boss for a moment before an-
swering. They had had other discussions about work
before; this certainly wasn't the first time Joe had solicited
his opinion about something. But he wondered what Joe
was really after. Was he annoyed about the heated exchange he and Barbara had at the meeting? Les wished he
could read Joe's mind before giving an answer.

"I'm glad we have them," Les finally said. "I think
we've all got a better sense of what's going on in the
company." He paused, sipped his beer, and then continued. "But there is something that bothers me. Those meetings can be stressful. You don't always want to risk expos-
ing yourself or knocking someone else's ideas, you
know?" He looked at Joe, a cautious smile forming on his
face. "Especially in front of the boss. Sometimes I wonder
whether everyone can really take part and get involved."

"You certainly speak up and get involved and I'm glad
you do."

Les was relieved. "That's me. I like to mix things up.
But it's hard to have the kind of good discussion that can
really help us settle things. Not everyone loves each other
or sees eye-to-eye in there."

They talked like this for awhile, with Les expressing his
concerns and reservations and Joe trying to be both supportive and objective. Finally, without really resolving the
matter, the two decided to call it a night. Driving home,
though, Joe seriously considered what Les had said.
"Yes," he admitted to himself, "the meetings serve a
purpose, but something is missing. Problems and opportunities float around us as they used to float around just
me. We don't really seize an issue, grapple with it, and
then move forward. Maybe the problems are just too
complex, too intractable. Or maybe it's us..."

Examining the Conflicts at Heart Tech

Conflict is a natural part of our lives. It is a common feature of work, politics, family life—indeed, every situation in which different people with differing goals and outlooks come together. Generally speaking, we seem to find conflict acceptable—we even expect it — outside of the workplace. It is strange, then, that we view conflict so negatively when it happens at the office. Yet the fact of the matter is this: Conflict can be your friend and your company's salvation. But you must understand and manage conflict to make it a positive organizational feature.

Conflict is very much a part of the life and problems at Heart Technologies. As Joe, Les, Barbara, Al, and Gary discuss issues, seek solutions, and work together, they clash and quarrel. They see problems from different perspectives, disagree over organizational priorities, and have divergent opinions on the best course the organization should take. They must learn to handle this conflict, for they cannot escape it.

Conflict doesn't occur because people are mean-spirited and narrow-minded; nor can conflicts be managed by asking everyone to be kind. Conflict is a natural part of working together to solve problems and get things done.

Unfortunately, people often work harder to forget about conflict than to learn from it. By examining in greater detail the conflicts that occurred at Heart Tech's management meeting, we can learn much about the managers as people, how they work together, and their effectiveness in dealing with conflict.

Joe and Brian

Joe believed that making managers a cohesive team was critical to the continued success of the company. Brian, however, didn't see things in the same light. Distrustful of team approaches to problems, he saw his role as developing high-quality, state-of-the-art products. They disagreed on the issue of Brian's participation on the management

group. Although he very much wanted Brian to participate in the management team, Joe knew that alienating
Brian would be counter-productive, perhaps even disas-
trously so, and he thus avoided straining their relationship. Joe was also reluctant to press his point because he
was not totally clear himself on the value to be gained by
Brian's participation, though he knew intuitively that such
value did exist, and doubted that he could present his
reasons convincingly.

But Joe's avoidance of this conflict, while understand-
able, was costly. In an open discussion, they could have
productively examined the pros and cons of Brian's involvement with the other managers. Joe could have clarified the need and advantages of this involvement. He
could have explained, for example, that as a living symbol
of the company and its high-quality products, Brian could
serve as a unifying force within the company. Such a role,
however, would require that he be more accessible.

Brian's work, meanwhile, would profit if he had a better
understanding of the perspectives, ideas, and agendas of
the other managers. The research and development group
is very important, but it has to develop products that
production can build, marketing can sell, and finance can
support. Les, for instance, has information about the needs
and desires of physicians and other customers that could
very well lead to profitable modifications and new products that would be important competitive advantages for
the company.

A more open discussion between Joe and Brian might
also have clarified for Joe any potential downsides of
Brian's involvement. Brian might be distracted from his
work, for example, or if he were to act arrogantly, he
might alienate the other managers. In either case, discussing the conflict would have allowed Brian and Joe to
become aware of the consequences of their present actions,
choose an approach they agreed to be the most useful, and
recognize what is needed to implement that approach.
Conflict, openly and constructively discussed, would help

them make free, informed decisions and act wisely. Without conflict, they are less motivated to understand the situation, less aware of alternatives, and less able to create more effective ways of working.

Les and Barbara

Les wanted to discuss the role of the new contracts administrator. Barbara asserted that such a discussion was premature.

It was Les's assumption that the management meeting was an appropriate time for such a probe, but when Barbara opposed it and he received no support from the others, he quickly retreated. He was not so confident of his own abilities or conclusions that he wanted to push ahead. Nor did he want to risk appearing to be a trouble-maker.

Barbara was ambivalent. At first she felt under attacked and feared Les might damage her stature among the other managers; but she quickly decided that Les meant no harm. She tried to assure everyone that she was not flustered. To show Les that she was not angry with him, she kidded him about his birthday.

As an observer, Joe knew that Barbara had cut Les short. Although he wanted to support Les, he did not want to appear to take sides or to push Barbara into a discussion she clearly didn't want. By attempting to be impartial, however, he gave the impression that he was siding with Barbara.

Their failure to examine Les's concerns could prove costly to the company. At his previous job with a computer manufacturer, Les watched a power struggle develop between the contracts administrator and the sales force. Neither the administrator nor the sales people were able to negotiate their differences. Both sides grew very angry, and complained about each other to top management. Management did not anticipate—nor was it equipped to cope with—the situation. All it could think of doing was firing the administrator, assuming that it would be easier to replace one individual than an entire sales staff. As a result, a potentially valuable employee was lost and what remained was a bitter and fragmented organizational atmosphere.

Les did not want to see this costly problem develop at Heart Tech. He did not have a concrete solution, but he believed that if management anticipated and prepared for the problems, much unhappiness and unproductive squabbling could be avoided. He hoped that discussion among the managers would get them all thinking about how to avoid a win-lose conflict between contracts and sales. Barbara, Joe, and the other Heart Tech managers avoided a potentially divisive conflict, and in so doing, risked a harmful, difficult-to-resolve conflict in the future.

Al and Les

Al and Les debated incentive programs openly and directly. When he believed he was right, Al did not hesitate to say so, and he believed he was right about individual incentives. Though at times he came across as stubborn and tiresome, no one perceived him as mean-spirited or devious. If nothing else, the other managers could simply say to themselves, "There he goes again," and nod in his direction, half-listening and half-planning an escape.

Les, still smarting from his run-in with Barbara, also held strong opinions on incentives. He said that Al's incentive scheme would be impractical and ineffective. He felt his adrenaline flow, but worried that he might appear overly emotional and that he was fighting too hard.

Despite Les's worries, though, a very useful purpose was served by the confrontation. Caught up in the excitement of the debate, the other managers were stirred to think of their own experiences and express their own ideas. They came to unsurprising but useful conclusions. If incentive plans were complex, developing new markets was even more so. The conflict made it clear to all managers that while Les and his sales staff could begin to solve the new-markets problem, everyone needed to collaborate on a marketing approach that would serve the whole company.

Conflict and Getting Things Done at Heart Tech

Though it is clear that the conflict between Al and Les had the potential, properly managed, to lead to something beneficial to everyone, it should not be assumed that conflict is uncomplicated. The Heart Tech managers, for example, are in conflict even over how they should manage their conflicts, and the personalities of those involved in any dispute plays an important part in how differences of opinion can be productively resolved. Les likes, as he says, to "mix things up." Barbara values a professional stoicism and an aura of control. Al will challenge others on issues he feels strongly about. Gary uses humor and a sharp-edged wit to express his views and feelings. Brian prefers to avoid discussion with the managers he doesn't know well. Joe facilitates discussion even when there is conflict, but also tries not to offend those who would rather avoid it. Once they all agree on constructive methods with which to discuss their disagreements, they can work more effectively together and function better as a team.

Although conflict is part of the problem, it is also very much a part of the solution. It is through their discussion of opposing views that Heart Tech managers can better understand their common goals. Through open and honest disagreement they can better explore the company's options, create new competitive advantages, update their procedures, and improve the way they work with each other. In the simplest terms, conflict itself is not a barrier to teamwork. Rather, conflict has the potential to turn a collection of individuals and departments into a cohesive, productive organization.

Dealing with Conflict at Heart Tech

Is conflict really so important for Heart Tech and its managers? They don't call each other's names, curse, swear, or throw fists; they may even seem like a harmonious group. Caustic comments, heated shouting matches, verbal duels, and violence, occur in many organizations, but they are only some forms of conflict. Frequently, conflict takes on a more subdued aspect, as it did at Heart Tech.

It is common to think that the approach of avoiding open discussion and downplaying differences generally used by Heart Tech managers demonstrates their competence and maturity. However, recent research strongly documents that avoiding conflict can be very destructive. Indeed, as we have seen the tendency to avoid conflict at Heart Tech can be much more costly than commonly recognized. Nor is avoiding conflict easy. Les, for example, has to work hard to disguise his feelings toward Barbara and her treatment of him. Despite his efforts, these feelings affected the way he discussed the incentives issue with Al. Les also began to doubt how effectively he could work with Barbara, and how effective the management meetings might be.

Avoiding conflict is popular despite its costs because many people do not have the values, skills, and procedures to discuss their differences openly and constructively. Conflict is traditionally thought to be necessarily destructive, something to be dispensed with rationally, coolly, and quickly. Many managers assume their role is to be in charge and, if any disagreement occurs, to end it decisively. "Being a team member" often means agreeing with the boss and not rocking the boat by dealing with the conflict openly. As Heart Tech managers will learn, it is not easy to break out of these traditional practices.

What the managers at Heart Tech must understand, as we shall see, is that they have more to gain by dealing openly with conflict than by avoiding and smoothing over their differences. They need to be sensitive to the many pressures on them to avoid conflict. Rather than smooth over, they need to make thoughtful decisions about how to handle conflict.

Once they decide to confront their differences, however, the managers must have the ability to discuss them thoroughly. Indeed, if they don't have the appropriate skills, they are apt to avoid open discussion or interact in a nonproductive manner. In the following chapters, we'll be looking at various examples of how conflict can be managed to everyone's benefit. By looking at events as they transpire at Heart Tech, we'll be able to suggest ideas, skills, and procedures that are useful for discussing conflicts openly and productively in a number of settings.

Chapter 2
Teamwork, Conflict, and Innovation

Gary Eckberg felt out of step with Joe lately. When he had joined the firm four years ago, Gary believed he could live with Joe's talk about a corporate family and teamwork; he simply dismissed it as window dressing. But now Joe seemed committed to make the talk a reality, and Gary thought that was a big mistake. He was cured of his enchantment with teamwork and corporate unity at CompDatum in Dallas. There was a big difference, he had learned, between the lip service management gave to team approaches and the insensitive way that conflict was really handled. But he didn't want to talk about his reservations or his experiences at CompDatum. Joe, he hoped, would soon get frustrated and become realistic. He was a little nervous, therefore, when Joe asked to meet to discuss his opinions on the management team and group incentives.

Joe escorted Gary into his office, but unable to think of any small talk or joke, he got down to business. "I've been thinking about incentives and teamwork," Joe said. "What we may need are incentives for the whole management team, perhaps for the entire company. There must be some research on this. What do you think about giving incentives to the whole group?"

"You're really going for this teamwork idea, aren't you?" Gary said with a tentative, cautious smile. He was trying to use humor as a screen that would protect him if Joe responded badly. He wanted to keep his feelings in check, but they pushed for expression. "Yeah, there's lots written about the problems with groups. Groups can be very conforming and restrictive. You've heard of groupthink, haven't you, or group tyranny? Or the joke about a camel being a horse designed by a committee? Groups are slow and cumbersome. Sometimes a manager has to be a leader and make the tough decisions."

"There are problems, I suppose," Joe countered. "But it seems to that there's lots of good things that groups do."

"People can let the other guy do it and then take the credit...you mean that sort of thing," Gary joked. He wanted to lighten the conversation, and maybe Joe's evangelism.

Joe smiled. "But people enjoy working with others. I know I'd be frustrated if I couldn't talk things over with other people. I don't like sitting alone in my office. And frankly, there are times when another perspective can open up a whole new way of looking at a problem."

"Wouldn't it be fairer to just say that some people like working in teams and can do well in that kind of situation? Lots of very bright, productive people want to keep a long way from meetings and groups. They are the stars, the hustlers who refuse to conform to the lowest common denominator. Put everyone into groups and there goes innovation. Look at Brian. Where would Heart Tech be without him?"

"Brian is creative, but he's not really a loner. He and the staff get together frequently. He talks to many other researchers...you should see his phone bill. He keeps talking about research synergy."

"Joe, why have you become so keen about all this corporate family and teamwork stuff?" Gary was caught up in the debate and was revealing much more than he had planned. "Just because a few books are written about it does not mean it's right for us."

Usually, Gary kept his discussions light; Joe was now seeing a new side of his colleague, and he was pleased. He found the intellectual give and take stimulating. "To me the need to work together is as plain as day," he said. "It's like the air we breathe; it's all around us and we need it."

"But Joe, you're so gung-ho."

"I don't think so. Look, our tenth anniversary is coming up. I want something to show for my efforts. For our efforts. I want us all to be proud of the company and to have the company make its mark. I want the company to be as good as it can be. Working together is the way to do it."

"Here's where I see things differently, I guess," Gary said deliberately. "At CompDatum we were all getting into this corporate family stuff. We had the Friday beer bashes, company tennis courts, and corporate celebrations... you should have seen the extravagant Christmas dinners. Dallas knows how to put on lavish affairs. One year we flew in a world famous Hong Kong chef, the next year a French one...crazy, wild stuff. We had a good thing going. But along came a dip in the market, and the wunderkind who was the force behind the company sold us to a Silicon Valley firm and cashed in his chips. He gave speeches about how the new management wanted to keep the team together, blah, blah, blah...But everything went downhill from there fast. The new company really wanted our technology, not our people. I saw the handwriting on the wall and left."

"I can see why you are a little skeptical about this family feeling," Joe said sympathetically, "But it sounds to me that the real problem was the sell-off, not the team approach, don't you think?"

Gary shrugged his shoulders noncommitally. He clearly wasn't convinced. "Maybe. I admit I was bitter—I guess I still am—but I've concluded that one should expect that sort of thing. This is business after all, and the point is to make money, not to be a family."

"But there's more than making money," Joe said.

"Sometimes you lose money—when the cost of French chefs is higher than your profits, for example," Gary joked.

"Seriously, Gary, I'm not interested in losing money, but I don't like the idea that all I'm doing is making a buck."

"What's wrong with that? Some of the nicest people are rich. I like my BMW, and you have a pretty nice new Caddy, I see."

"Just making money never had a great appeal to me, and less now." Joe was a little annoyed at Gary's off-handed jab. "Since my father died last July, I have been thinking about how fragile life is. He was in robust health, still young at 68. All of a sudden a heart attack, and he's gone."

"That's a much different matter," Gary conceded.

"It is? I'm not so sure. I feel much closer to my own mortality. My father was the buffer between me and death. No," he said, anticipating the comment he could see forming on Gary's face, "I'm not being morbid. His death made me much more interested in living. And much more conscious of what has real value in life. It's not enough for me to struggle and be successful for the future. The future is now."

"I can see why you feel more dedicated," Gary acknowledged. He tried to get them back to their original subject. "But that still doesn't mean that group incentives and teamwork are the way to go. A strong company is built on the independent, creative efforts of individuals. Emphasize groups and out goes the hard-driving, motivated winners, those guys who want to be recognized for their own efforts, not for being on a team. And who will be left? The losers."

"The world is not divided into winners and losers," Joe replied. "Most people want to do a good job, but they need help. I need help; you need help. Isn't that the essence of teamwork?"

"This group thing is too much. Look at all the problems. People fight and argue, and then compromise. Never mind that one side might be right and the other wrong. To avoid an ugly confrontation, they settle on something in the middle, a lowest common denominator. Well, the truth is never in the middle. People don't want to go to meeting after meeting. What's more, most people couldn't work in a group if their life depended upon it!"

"You've got a point there," Joe said. He was impressed by the intensity of Gary's feelings. "People must know how to work in groups. If they don't know how, then we need to teach them to communicate and handle their problems and conflicts."

"Do you think people can learn to handle conflict? Most people don't, and will never be able to."

"Sure they can. We handle conflicts all the time; it's part of everyday life. Even the two of us right now are handling conflict; we're discussing our opposing views about groups and teamwork. Hey," Joe said, smiling, "We aren't doing such a bad job."

Gary hesitated. "It's not the most fun I've had all week, but I guess we are exchanging views."

"I feel I understand you better now, Gary. In a way, I think I understand myself better. I'm not sure I agree with you, at least not on everything, but you've helped me see more clearly what's involved in teamwork. Effective teams just don't happen; people must learn how to use them to make them work."

Teamwork and Conflict

Joe and Gary used their conflict to express their opinions and explore each other's thinking. Gary talked about his painful experience at CompDatum. Joe revealed personal attitudes that influenced his management approach. They acknowledged the barriers to making teamwork a reality. Teamwork must be well managed. People must be able to discuss the inevitable frustrations, difficulties, and differences of opinions that arise when they work together.

Their divergent attitudes toward conflict led to their disagreement on teamwork. To Gary, groups demand conformity and suppress individuality: The energy of the creative few is dispersed by the less able; the vision of the brilliant is diluted by the near-sightedness of the average. Even bright people, he assumed, find it difficult to disagree, and must silently give in to group pressure. It was his experience that conflicts are seldom positively handled because few people have or can learn the skills to manage conflict.

In contrast, Joe assumed that persons working together will help more than frustrate each other. He was not so naive as to believe that there is no conflict in collaboration, but he thought people could work out their difficulties and use their opposing views and ideas productively. Joe believed that people can express themselves openly and solve their problems better together than alone.

Because they took a useful approach to discussing their opposing views, Joe and Gary came to agree that managing conflict-not the absence of conflict-is crucial for productive teamwork. They strongly defended their own positions, but they largely avoided the 'I'm right, you're wrong' arguments that would have turned the disagreement into a confrontation of egos and personalities rather than ideas and perceptions. They sought to find out what is right rather than who is right. Recognizing that the truth seldom resides solely with one person, they dug into the issue at hand. They listened and accepted each other's arguments, and put them together to deepen their understanding.

Conflict and Management Innovations

Joe began to see that managing conflict makes an organization work. To compete successfully—to take advantage of new technologies, respond to consumer demands, and gain the commitment of the people working with and for them—Joe and other managers today are experimenting with participative management to involve employees and develop strong corporate cultures to bind them together into a cohesive, productive workforce. Project teams of designers, engineers, environmentalists, construction specialists, accountants, and administrators are expected to work together to build a new transmission line. Task forces with representatives from all departments recommend ways to improve coordination between departments. Assembly line workers form work groups to assemble an automobile engine that will perform well. Machine operators meet regularly to discuss how to increase productivity. Labor-management groups improve the quality of work life.

Conflict is much more fundamental to these management innovations than is commonly recognized. It should surprise no one that different departments often seem to have their own agendas; it is not unusual for there to be a certain degree of adversarial feeling in their interactions, a kind of my turf/your turf undercurrent. However, employees, departments, and business units must all work together and share their expertise to make the organization more productive and humane. Even the most groundbreaking invention in the world risks not seeing the light of day unless R&D, marketing, finance, production, and everyone else in the company works together in concert. And productive management of conflict is absolutely essential if people and groups are to collaborate.

Traditional organizations are based on the belief that conflict is destructive. Appalled at the confusion in the organizations of their time, Fredrick Taylor and other early theorists wanted efficiency and rationality, and proposed organizations that would minimize conflict and give managers the clout to end conflict. Individuals should work alone to avoid wasting their time coordinating and disagreeing, they believed. Rules and procedures should make all coordination routine and efficient. Personal feelings and attitudes should not interfere with following procedures. When procedures were incomplete or employees failed to follow them, managers must end the conflict by making a decision.

The Traditional Organization

The underlying assumption is that conflict is negative and potentially very harmful so that it must be minimized or quickly stopped.

- Tasks assigned to individuals; individuals are the basic building blocks of organizations.
- Written rules and procedures to coordinate.
- Impersonal relationships to minimize the effects of emotions.
- Managerial leaders who make decisions and solve problems decisively.

The Contemporary Organization

The underlying assumption is that conflict is potentially very productive, but must be used skillfully to realize this potential.

- Tasks assigned to groups; groups are the basic building block of the organization.
- Team meetings to decide how to work together and resolve problems.
- Genuine, open relationships in which employees express their feelings, hunches, and frustrations.
- Participative leaders who involve and discuss the problems and conflicts openly and constructively.

Contemporary managers are challenging these traditional assumptions, however, especially the notion that conflict is destructive. They seek genuine, open relationships. "Business-like" relationships in which people try to hide their frustration and affection are unrealistic and undesirable. Recognizing the value of human resources and the importance of a common purpose and a shared vision, companies care about their employees as individuals and want them to care for each other.

Similarly, the participative manager is replacing the traditional "decisive" manager who sets goals and gets subordinates to accomplish them. The modern manager involves employees in the activities of the department. Employees provide information and perspectives that improve decisions; they feel more valued and appreciated by contributing to the company.

Conflict is neither hero nor villain; people make conflict constructive or destructive. Strong corporate cultures, interdisciplinary task forces, and other new ways of working do not by themselves make a company flexible and productive. Research indicates that to make participation work, managers and employees must be able to discuss their opposing ideas. But organizations are in transition now, and traditional attitudes interfere. Employees have been told for years to be rational and task oriented. Managers have been told they must keep their group harmonious and end problems decisively. Conflict is still equated with confusion and disruption.

New ways of working require productive conflict. Conflict provides the energy that drives these practices and makes them work. Through conflict, people express their positions, identify obstacles and opportunities, learn from each other, and devise new ways of working. Managers and employees who are locked into the traditional ways of doing things lack healthy, productive ways of managing differences, and in this kind of environment, conflict can erupt to tear organizations apart and make exchange impossible.

Chapter 3
Approaches to Conflict

After a day working with other executives to create jobs for minority Americans, Joe turned his thoughts again to his management team. He saw Les and called out, "Les, can you step into my office for a minute?" Not wishing to appear severe, he smiled and added, "When you have time, that is."

Les, still somewhat anxious about talking to his new boss, even after the conversation they had at Pete's Pub, welcomed the opportunity. He wanted to be useful to the company, and Joe was both open and powerful. "Sure, be there in a minute." Les got his notebook from his desk, took a moment to collect his thoughts, and set off for Joe's office.

Directing Les to a chair in the sitting area of the office, Joe said, "I've been meaning to talk to you about your volleyball playing. Aren't you a little too aggressive out there...I thought we had hired a nice guy to be our marketing manager. You get on a court, and all of a sudden you become Rambo or something."

"You've got to be merciless out there." Les joined in the fun. "This is supposed to be to a progressive company in a progressive community. Now I'm finding that it's cut-throat. It's a dog-eat-dog world around here, no doubt about it."

"I didn't lay it on that thick, did I?" Joe asked. When he first interviewed Les for his job, he had talked about the quality of life and progressive traditions in Minnesota and Heart Tech's efforts to create a family spirit. Joe wanted people who would like working in such an environment. Yet he couldn't help feeling a little corny talking like that to someone he didn't know. He wondered if he appeared naive and sentimental.

"No, no..." Les was glad to be off to a good start.

"Listen, here's what I really want to talk to you about. You said something after the game on Wednesday that got me thinking. I want our management meetings to make us a winning team. I know we must work hard to succeed. We touch base at the meetings, we communicate, but I don't think we're really able to wrestle with issues and solve problems."

"One problem is time," Les replied. "Meetings fly by. We've got so much to cover that we're always in a hurry. We can't really dig into things. I know I check myself before raising an issue or making a point by asking myself, 'Do we have time for this?' and often the answer is 'No'."

"We do need more time." Joe realized as he talked, however, that more time was an incomplete remedy.

"If the problem is important, we all want to take the time to discuss it."

"Something else you said seems to tie into all of this, something about how we don't see eye to eye on these matters. You weren't saying that we can't be a team?"

"We can be a team, but we have different views and styles. It takes time to understand each other and work together."

Glancing at the ceiling, Joe paused then said, "Gary and I just talked about this yesterday. I'm not so worried that we have different ideas. But we have different styles. That strikes me as the important thing. We all have our own way of talking—or not talking—about issues and conflict."

"We're individuals," Les said. He wanted to be more specific, but he held back. He was reluctant to name names because he didn't want to appear as if he was talking behind his colleagues' backs.

Joe liked talking about other people, however. He thought for a moment before saying anything. He didn't want to give the impression that he was going to make critical comments to Les about the other team members. "I know what you mean. Take Barbara. She's very competent and strong, and handles herself well. She's certainly not overly emotional. But I think she has trouble dealing with problems in a group setting. She doesn't like to get involved in heated discussions. I'm not criticizing her, of course: that's her style and we should recognize it."

"Barbara does seem to have some 'professor' in her," Les agreed. "Slugging it out in the trenches is not really her thing."

"Now Al," Joe continued, "is really a nice guy, but getting into a debate with him can be exasperating."

"I know. I found that out at the last meeting. Scratch him a little, and out he comes. But he stings like a butterfly really."

"One thing about Al, though, is that he bounces back. He might be pinned into a corner, but he keeps on making his points. But debating Al can be no fun. He digs in his heels, and insists that he's right. Though I suppose I get as stubborn as he is."

"Uh, no comment," Les said with a grin. "Gary's different from both of them. He takes everything pretty cool. He always has something funny to say, regardless of how tense things get."

"I enjoy his humor," Joe said, "But I wish he would be more serious at times. Well, like we said, we all have our own way of discussing things. Myself, I feel torn because I want to talk about these problems and work out solutions, but I know that we have time constraints and not everyone wants to talk. I don't want to be heavy-handed and force people to talk. But I want to be the leader of an effective team. It's difficult to know what to do."

"I think we need to agree on how we're going to operate. Perhaps we should sit down and think about how we're going to discuss issues and handle conflicts."

"I like that," Joe said sincerely. "You can help us get better at talking about problems. You like to mix things up, talk about conflicts directly. We need that."

"Thanks. I'm not sure I'm that good. But I agree that we'll be better off talking about our differences instead of pretending they don't exist."

Ways to Manage Conflict

Joe and Les recognized that they must learn to use conflict. Open discussions of contentious issues invigorates the managers at Heart Tech, enabling them to explore and identify issues and solve problems. They feel powerful and in control of their company's future as they anticipate and overcome obstacles. Conflict can disrupt relationships, organizations, and even societies. But conflict itself does not destroy. It is how people approach and handle their conflicts that can be disastrous. What are the approaches that realize the potential and reduce the costs of conflict?

Managers at Heart Tech used many strategies in conflict. They asked questions, made jokes, told others they were wrong, reiterated their position, and kept quiet. People are very creative in their use of conflict strategies. They can compromise, reassure, propose, demand, threaten, problem solve, shout, withdraw, plead, yell,

storm, give in, and cry. They are cold and harsh, tough
and mean, or warm and soft. They can raise their eyebrows, clench their fists, or grin and bear their frustration.
Moreover, people combine strategies in complex ways.
They may first cajole, then threaten, then plead, and
finally cry. People use silence as well as violence; they
tease as well as punish.

This great variety of strategies makes conflict interesting, but it also makes documenting positive ways to
manage conflict difficult. However, research has identified
four contrasting approaches that very much affect how
conflict is managed. These approaches are based on the
intentions of those involved a given dispute. One intention
is whether people want to talk about conflict directly or
avoid and smooth over differences. The second intention
is whether people want to discuss the issues for common
benefit or to pursue their own interests and goals at
others' expense.

Four Approaches to Conflict

	WIN/LOSE	MUTUAL
A V O I D	GOSSIP REVENGE SABOTAGE	HUMOR CONCILIATORY HELPFUL
O P E N	ARGUMENT THREATEN STRUGGLE TO WIN	GIVE AND TAKE DISCUSSION PROBLEM SOLVE

Open and Avoid

Do people try to discuss the conflict directly or do they want to avoid such a discussion and quickly smooth over their differences? The difference often determines whether the conflict takes a productive or destructive course. Heart Tech managers were sometimes willing to air their differences openly, at other times not. Les, for example, concluded that Barbara did not want to talk about the contracts administrator and that she might make it painful for him to try. Al and Les, on the other hand, indicated that they wanted an open discussion and they quickly joined into a debate on incentive plans. Likewise, Gary and Joe openly discussed their opposing views on teamwork and group incentives.

Open discussion conveys the desire to communicate one's feelings, goals, and hopes; it says you are willing to take the risks to let others know what you are feeling and thinking and that you are equally willing to listen to their opinions. Openness is an attempt to develop ideas and possible solutions to problems, and to motivate others to do something about the problem.

In contrast, avoiding conflicts conveys a desire to hide your feelings, a lack of confidence in your position and reasoning, and perhaps even doubt that the problem is important enough to warrant discussion and risk arousing animosity. Things can go on as before, avoidance seems to suggest, and there is little need to change. Avoidance can communicate that there is no conflict.

Mutual and Win-Lose

People approach conflict with a particular aim: To work it out for mutual benefit or to assert their interests and position at the expense of others. Simply stated, they can take a win-win or a win-lose view of the conflict. Research has documented that mutual approaches to conflict are productive, and that win-lose are destructive. (It should be acknowledged that sometimes people aren't sure themselves what their intentions are. A manager might believe that his or her aims are purely altruistic when in fact they are not. For this reason, it makes sense for people involved in conflict to be open and honest with themselves about what they're after and what is really at stake.)

Al and Les discussed the incentive plans in largely a win-lose way. Each became committed to showing that his position was right and the other's wrong; each attempted to assert his position over the other's. However, Barbara, Gary, and Joe turned the discussion so that the objective was to develop a solution that would be best for all.

Pursuing mutual benefit (win-win) implies that people will work together to solve their common problem; solutions should be useful for all. Since everyone shares in the problem, everyone can be part of the solution. The conflict will proceed on the understanding that everyone can contribute to the solution, that all will express their opinions and make suggestions, and that the best ideas will be put together to solve the problem. Win-lose intentions, however, imply that someone may be blamed for the problem and that one position will be asserted over others. People assume there will be a winner and a loser and they want to be a winner.

These intentions yield four major approaches to managing conflict: (1) avoid discussing conflicts and pursue mutual benefit, (2) avoid discussion and pursue your own interests at another's expense, (3) discuss issues openly in a win-lose way, (4) discuss conflicts openly for joint benefit. Managers and employees alike must be able to approach their conflicts in all four ways and decide which approach is the most useful under the particular circumstances. Let's take a closer look at how managers can carry out these approaches and review what research has shown about when the respective approaches are most useful.

Communicating Your Approach

What is key to remember is that your intention and the approach you want to use are not always the intention and approach others believe you are taking. The effect and success of any approach depends on how others view and interpret it. What counts is not the actions taken by one person or the approach taken, but the conclusions and reactions of others. People want to know what others are trying to accomplish. On the basis of their understanding, they respond and carry on with the conflict.

To understand the implications of this, think back to the exchange between Les and Barbara at the first meeting. Les thought he was trying to discuss the conflict about Richard, the contracts administrator, in an open, mutual way. But Barbara suspected that Les was taking a win-lose approach to make her look ineffective for failing to handle Richard. Based on this conclusion, she reacted defensively. Without any chance for clarifying their respective positions and intentions, the two would quickly reach an impasse, the problem would remain unsolved, and in all likelihood Les and Barbara would wind up being somewhat distrustful of each other.

Miscommunication is common in conflict. People who argue their own positions aggressively or feel strongly about the conflict are often thought to be pursuing their interests at the expense of others. People who want to dig into the problem are seen as accusatory or judgmental. Persons who are nervous about initiating a discussion are assumed to want to avoid open conflict. Because intentions are so easily miscommunicated in conflict, people must use overlapping ways to communicate what they are trying to do.

There are two primary ways by which intentions are communicated. The first happens prior to the conflict and has to do with the attitudes and relationship already developed. If an open and mutually trusting relationship already exists between them, the people involved in the conflict are less likely to see things in an adversarial or personal light. The second way to communicate intentions concerns the strategy and actions taken in dealing with the conflict. Strategy alone does not communicate intentions, of course. The effects of any strategy depend upon the attitudes people have toward each other. People interpret and react differently to a warning from an aloof boss than they do from a close friend. To communicate an intention accurately, the relationship developed before the conflict and the strategies used during the conflict must complement each other. Once again, you must be willing to honestly and critically evaluate what kind of relationship you have with those you are in conflict with or whose conflict you are mediating.

We can better see how this works by looking at each strategy separately.

Open Discussion

Before the Conflict. Sharing information with others, asking for their opinions, listening carefully to them, showing concern for their feelings, and demonstrating a willingness to do something about problems all contribute to a productive climate. Open door policies, the use of team meetings, and participative management convey the message that persons should discuss problems and conflicts openly.

During the Conflict. People can indicate openness during the conflict in many ways. The most common is to present your own views in a way that clearly shows you expect others will express theirs. It must be remembered, however, that it is not enough for you to be open in expressing your positions; you must create an environment that encourages others to express theirs. A tough, closed-minded boss may be quite open with his opinions, while at the same time conveying that it is risky for employees to disagree. Two-way openness, as its name suggests, implies a willingness to listen to others as well as to disclose your own feelings and ideas.

Avoidance

People have many ways of making it known that conflict should be avoided and smoothed over. Not talking about the subject, smiling on the outside while crying or cursing on the inside, and assuring the other that there is no problem at all, are straightforward ways to smooth over conflict. Similarly, much energy and skill go into creating a great variety of impressive, skillful ways to avoid conflict. Too bad this energy isn't channelled into managing conflict productively!

Before the Conflict. An organizational culture that sends out the message that conflict is destructive or that the relationship is not strong enough to withstand conflict, makes open discussions appear risky. Unspoken or hidden messages—the messages conveyed by tone of voice or body language—that communicate that conflict must be avoided include:

"I am weak and fragile, please don't pick a fight with me."

"I am stressed and overworked, please don't do this to me."

"I am so busy that I don't have time to talk about that now."

"I am so important that I cannot be bothered with something so mickey mouse."

"First we will thoroughly discuss whether we have the right kind of pencils, whether everyone is satisfied with the coffee machine, and what people's reactions are to the new stationery. Then we'll squeeze in a minute or two on whether we should reorganize the department."

During the Conflict. People develop many different ways to deflect and smooth over conflict:

"That's an interesting point, but now is not the time to discuss it."

"It just happens that way, and I don't think it is worth getting heated up about."

"Let's cooperate rather than bicker."

"Life is never a bowl of cherries."

"It will be ok tomorrow."

"You are young and new to the organization...you'll get used to how we do things here."

"Let's be reasonable and rational, and not let emotions take over."

"I want to hear what you are saying" while looking at the clock.

"I want to hear what's on your mind" while getting tense and hostile.

(Of course, there are times when a discussion of problems can't take place or when emotions should be given a cooling-off period. But unless the reasons for deferring discussion are reasonable and made clear, the message that you'll be sending is that you are not willing to deal with conflict.)

Mutual Interests

Before the Conflict. In a Mutual Interest strategy, people understand that they are working together and fairly share the benefits of their collaboration. They expect everyone will gain from a solution to any problem or conflict. Prior success in working with each other helps to establish this outlook. When employees have achieved common goals, know each other as people, are positively oriented toward each other, communicate accurately, and are open to each other, they are apt to discuss problems and conflicts and are prepared to meet any test that conflict brings.

During the Conflict. People express their feelings and views fully, listen closely to each other, share responsibility for the problem, define the problem to everyone's satisfaction, create solutions that combine the best ideas of all, select a solution that furthers the important interests of everyone, and distribute tasks to implement the solution.

Win-Lose

Before the Conflict. Many people assume that all disagreement and conflict is a competitive, win-lose struggle. It is easy to convince others that one is pursing one's interests at their expense. Unless provided clear evidence to the contrary, they expect that in conflict others are trying to outdo them, show them up, and force them to accept an unsatisfactory agreement. People who have competed against each other are especially prone to assume that what helps the other must harm them.

During the Conflict. Strategies that communicate a win-lose intention include: Making high initial demands and compromising slowly; concentrating on the strengths of your own position and the weakness of others; emphasizing the value of your own compromises while discounting those of the others; arguing that since others are to blame for the problem they should pay for the solution; trying to convince others that you are prepared to hold out for a maximally beneficial solution; and pressuring others to give into your demands. Deception, misleading information, coercion, and stubbornness are common competitive conflict strategies.

Consequences of Conflict Approaches

A great deal of research conducted by many social scientists indicates that open discussion of conflict for mutual, cooperative benefit is the most productive approach in most situations. It is critical that managers and employees discuss their conflicts openly and seek win-win solutions.

Avoid and Open Discussion

To avoid discussing conflict seems reasonable in the short run; however, it can undercut people's ability to work together and can be extremely costly. Avoiding conflict makes it difficult to solve problems and make decisions. People who avoid or smooth over their differences do not communicate their ideas and feelings accurately. They assume they understand each other, and have no way to check whether they actually do. If they falsely assume that they have the same perspective, they may feel good about this apparent harmony but they find themselves unprepared when the problem reappears. Conversely, if they assume their positions are totally incompatible, they will conclude they must work separately or against each other, thereby missing opportunities to collaborate.

Consequences of Four Approaches

	WIN/LOSE	MUTUAL
A V O I D	ILLUSION OF UNDERSTANDING PROBLEM UNSOLVED BITTERNESS	ILLUSION OF UNDERSTANDING SIMPLE SOLUTION FRIENDLINESS
O P E N	SOME ISSUES IDENTIFIED PROBLEM INTENSIFIED HOSTILITY	ISSUES IDENTIFIED CREATIVE SOLUTION CONFIDENCE AND CLOSENESS

Discussion helps people understand each other and combine their ideas and insights to create solutions to problems. Through open discussion, people check their misunderstandings and develop insight. However, open discussion does not itself result in accurate communication, strengthened relationships, and effective solutions. The discussion must be skillfully carried out. Throughout the rest of this book, we'll look more closely at what is involved in the successful management of conflict-based discussions. What is most critical is to convey that you want to work out the conflict for mutual benefit.

Mutual Interests and Win-Lose

Conveying the message that one wants to help everyone achieve their objectives contributes greatly to successful conflict management. People who believe they are trying to solve their conflicts for mutual, cooperative benefit develop a supportive climate that encourages everyone to talk accurately about their ideas, positions, and feelings. They then understand each other's point of view and perspective, and recognize similarities as well as differences. They are willing to respond to each other's needs, define the issue as a problem to be jointly solved, and combine the best ideas to adopt solutions that help everyone. They develop high morale and the confidence to discuss and solve future difficulties.

Pursuing your interest at the expense of others, however, creates a much different scenario. People who compete in conflict become suspicious and restrict their communication to that which favors their position. They emphasize their differences and incompatibilities, intensify the discussion, and increase the number of issues at stake. They soon believe that the conflict is either to be won or lost, and to win they must force their position. Either they will be unable to reach an agreement or someone in a position of authority will impose a solution. In either case, they are hostile and skeptical that they can work together in the future.

Although research indicates that an open, mutual discussion has the most potential benefits, findings do not indicate that managers must always discuss conflict in this way. Sometimes this approach is not desirable; the stronger relationships and problem solving of open, mutual discussion are not needed. Sometimes this approach is not workable; people do not have the skills to discuss their conflict cooperatively. Sometimes the approach is not efficient; it takes more time and energy than the benefits warrant. Managers must be flexible and choose the approach that is useful and workable for the specific conflict they face. However, it is the open, mutual approach that is the most productive and is now very much underused. The chapters to follow show managers how to use this approach to make conflict productive.

Chapter 4
Fighting Together

"Les, I've been thinking about what you said at the meeting," Barbara said when she ran into Les in the hallway. "You may have a point about Richard and the sales reps. I don't have anything concrete, but there seem to be some pretty negative attitudes."

Although she had at first dismissed them, Les' concerns about the new contracts administrator had alerted her to a potential problem. She no longer was amused when Richard joked about how he had to watch the sales staff before they gave the company away. She also wanted to show Les that she was not closed-minded and heard him at the management meeting.

Les was relieved that Barbara saw the problem, and recognized, though belatedly, his good intentions. "I don't have that much evidence either. I can tell you why I'm concerned." Les recalled that at his previous company the contracts administrator and sales people worked against each other. The administrator was eventually blamed and fired, but management had failed to help sales understand

the administrator's role or help them work out
their differences.

"I can see why you are concerned," Barbara said
somberly. They sat down in Barbara's office and talked
about what they could do.

"Perhaps the problem is that sales has to charge
Richard's time to its budget," Barbara suggested. "Joe and
I thought that contracts is a marketing cost and should be
part of the sales budget. But that may get Richard and the
sales reps off to a bad start. Maybe Richard should be a
corporate expense."

"That could help," Les said. His desultary manner
indicated he felt the budget issue was an incomplete
answer. "To tell you the truth, I'm not so sure what can be
done. I don't know enough about the problem to know
our options."

"There may be no simple solution...unfortunately."
Barbara felt that they were shooting in the dark.

"Maybe we could have Richard explain his purpose and
function to the sales people very clearly and carefully, so
that they all know what he is trying to do and can understand where he is coming from," Les offered.

"That could help," Barbara said. They both laughed as
they realized she had repeated Les' unenthusiastic re-
sponse to her suggestion. They agreed to give the matter
more thought and to get together with Joe.

Joe was pleased that Barbara and Les were talking.
More talking among the managers, he thought, was a
major purpose of the management meetings. He was
relieved because he remembered that when Barbara had
cut Les off at the meeting he had done nothing.

"I'm glad the two of you have overcome your rivalry on
the volleyball court to work together," Joe greeted Barbara
and Les. "Fill me in on where you are so far."

"It's not a big problem," Barbara began, "At least not
yet. But I think Les and I feel that we need to do

something about Richard's role and function. "There are bad attitudes brewing and we want to do something before the problem does get big."

"Richard and the sales representatives grumble about each other," Les continued. "Sales think he's too rigid, and Richard thinks the sales reps are too careless."

"I remember when we developed Richard's position," Barbara spoke to Joe. "You liked my idea that we needed to protect ourselves against very expensive litigation. Companies were losing millions in lawsuits; some went bankrupt because they were liable for more than they were worth. It seemed to make sense to have someone who would be solely responsible for protecting us. He would be a check against excess. All the contracts would have to be cleared through him before I would sign off and give the go ahead."

"It seemed like such a simple solution, but maybe it's not," Joe said. "What else can we do? We still think protection against lawsuits is a good idea, don't we?"

"Oh, yes, we have to be careful. Sales people realize that, though they may not be as committed and knowledgeable as we would like," Les added.

"We may want to make Richard's expenses a corporate one rather than make the sales reps charge it off on their budget. That would remove one source of irritation," Barbara said. "Les suggested that Richard should clearly inform the sales reps what his function is."

"I was thinking that maybe you and Barbara could both be there and tell sales the importance of Richard's role for the company," Les elaborated on his idea. "Richard's not just doing his thing, he's working for the company."

"Both ideas seem reasonable. What do sales and Richard think?" Joe asked.

"We've both talked to our people about the problem, but I have nothing concrete," Barbara said.

"Me neither," Les said. "I just talked casually to some of

the sales reps. I didn't want to call a special meeting to gripe about Richard."

"It seems like we are casting around for a solution without having much to go on," Joe said. "Rather than try to hammer out something here, doesn't it make sense to get the sales reps, Richard, and us all together? Isn't it more likely that we can really understand the problem and get a solution if all of us try to work out something?"

"Participation in action," Barbara said with a smile. "Might getting them all together make things worse, though? They could really be angry afterwards."

"Possibly," Les replied. "But the sales reps and Richard are sensible and reasonable. If they were already hostile, the meeting might be more difficult. But I think they'll welcome the meeting. They don't want a problem any more than we do."

"Its worth a try...it seems to make sense," Barbara said. She had her reservations, but she also thought that it might work. And she would learn more about managing and participation.

Barbara and Les discussed how to proceed. They agreed Joe shouldn't be there because Richard and the sales reps might be reluctant to discuss their difficulties openly in front of the CEO. John Buchan and Roger Cumberland were selected to represent sales because having the whole sales group there might intimidate Richard. John and Roger were reasonable people who had the confidence of the other sales people and seemed to get along well enough with Richard. Frankly, Barbara was surprised that Richard, John, and Roger welcomed the meeting.

Barbara and Les planned to make it clear they were united in wanting a workable solution that would help both Finance and Marketing. They wanted a genuine discussion to dig into the problem and generate new solutions. Barbara would begin the meeting because she could make specific preparation. Les would act as a facilitator during the discussion.

Barbara opened the meeting. "We're here to look at Richard's role, specifically how he can best work with the sales reps. We don't think there's a big problem now, but we want to prevent one from developing. This is not a 'who's fault is it' session. Les and I have no preconceived ideas about what the solution should be. We want your ideas and a full discussion of views. Richard, could you begin?"

"When Barbara approached me about this meeting, I didn't see the need," Richard said. "To tell the truth, I assumed from the start that I'd be in conflict with the sales reps...that was part of the job. But then I thought we should see if we could come up with a good way of working together."

"I believe I can speak for the sales reps," John spoke up. "We want to work better with Richard. Our jobs are difficult enough as it is. We don't need problems from our own people."

"We need to work together," Roger reinforced John.

"It's good we're on the same wavelength. Let's talk about what's going on now to get a better idea of what's happening," Les suggested. "Roger, what gets in the way of your working with Richard? What are the problems?"

"Well," Roger began hesitantly, "it's hard to pin down exactly, but there is something about Richard's attitude." Richard started to respond to this, but Les held up his hand, signalling to Richard that his turn would come. "He may understand our job, but he doesn't really appreciate the obstacles we face. What really galls us is when we work hard to develop a new client, he seems so skeptical—like he's sorry we got a new customer. It's easy for him to say, 'No! We must protect the company.' It's no trouble for him, but it's a big headache for us."

"That's not true," Richard broke in quickly. "I don't like saying no, but I've got my job, too. We can't give the company away just to get a few more customers. We have to balance sales against potential devastating legal action.

Everyone has to understand that."

"Yes, but we're the ones out there in the trenches every-day trying to get the customer, and then we have to come home to fight you," John defended Roger and sales. "You can have a pure attitude, but we have to cultivate new customers. We're not the only company in the market, you know."

The battlelines were quickly drawn. Richard, John, and Roger had strong feelings, and presented their views earnestly. Barbara wanted to intervene, but she remembered Les's advice that they should let them talk and only try to divert the discussion if it was really negative. The twenty-five minutes seemed like five minutes to Richard, John, and Roger and an hour to Barbara.

"OK, now we all know why we are having this meeting," Les said laughing. Roger, John, and Richard managed slight smiles. "We have negative friction and conflict here. There's an us-against-them attitude with everybody questioning everybody else's motives. Wouldn't you agree, Barbara?"

"I didn't realize there were such strong feelings," Barbara said. She wondered if there were other issues that bothered people much more than she had suspected.

"Well, I'm glad we got this out into the open. I think we all have a better understanding of the problem and each other's feelings. But what should we do about it?" Les said.

"It's easy to blame personalities in a situation like this, I guess," Roger began. "We can say that Richard is too rigid or whatever, and he has things to say about us...like we are reckless fools ready to forfeit the company for a commission. We know more stereotypes of sales reps than anyone; we've heard them for years. But I don't think that's it. We have the company's interests at heart and I'm sure Richard does too. It just that the way things are set up we fight against each other."

"Les and I have talked about what could be done,"

Barbara said. "We haven't come up with any set solution, though. And we wanted to get all your input first. But we had one idea. Perhaps charging Richard to the sales budget might be getting in your way. Les thought that having Richard explain his position and making it clear how it fits into the total picture might help."

John, Roger, and Richard all indicated that these steps seemed reasonable.

"I think we need more ideas." Les wanted to keep generating solutions.

"You know what gets in the way?" Roger said. "I think the sales people are upset because of the assumption that we're reckless, that we have to be checked up on, as if we don't give a damn about the company." He turned to Barbara and Les. "You want us out there building the company up, but you don't trust us to represent the company. We sign clients, but then we have to back down from appearing to represent the company. We feel like lackeys who have to get approval and OK from others. It makes us feel like children and we don't like that. And it's bad for the company, too, because it makes us look bad to our clients, like our own company doesn't trust us."

"That's a problem," Richard said sincerely. "I don't want you to think that I want you to appear weak. The company, including me, depends upon you guys. Still, we need to watch for legal problems."

"Perhaps Richard could advise and educate us rather than check up on us," John offered. "If you gave us guidelines and seminars on potential dangers, that would help us make sales to the people who can use our products. Believe it or not, we don't want to sell the products to people who can't use it and will give the company a bad name."

"Yeah, that could work. I like it," Richard said enthusiastically. "I could make explicit which customers worry us. We could have informal seminars to understand basic problems. I can do research to identify who is and who is not a risky customer."

"You would be a resource person we could talk to if the customer was really on the borderline," Roger said.

They discussed how Richard could help the sales reps become more aware of contract problems and more successfully market Heart Tech products.

"OK! We're getting somewhere now," Les said. "These ideas make the sales reps and Richard more of a team. You guys are working together rather than against each other."

"I feel that way too," Richard said. "I can do things that actually help sell our products."

"Richard could help Marketing in more general ways, too," Roger said. "Indicating that our products need a high level of expertise can be a marketing advantage. It can add prestige to buying our products. 'You have to be good to use Heart Tech.' Emphasizing our high standards and making them explicit could really reinforce that in the marketplace."

"Richard could help us find ways to help our customers get the expertise to use our products," John added. "I know health maintenance organizations that want to do more advanced surgery in-house, but they need more expertise and would welcome knowledge about how they could acquire it. Richard could help us establish ways they can develop the expertise. That would give us another edge in the marketplace."

"I feel like a fresh breeze has gone through my life." Richard was relieved and optimistic.

They talked more about how they could use their ideas.

"Very interesting and informative session," Barbara said as the room became quiet with everyone thinking about what had been said. "We're on a good track here."

"Perhaps we should close the meeting," Les suggested. "We should keep talking, and follow up on these ideas, though. Let's get back together in a couple of weeks and see what progress has been made."

John, Roger, and Richard identified times they could meet to get more concrete.

After the others had left, Barbara said to Les, "That was really great. We're off to an excellent start. I was impressed with everyone. Letting people talk and find solutions to problems can work. You ran it very well, Les, but you didn't dominate at all."

"Thanks, I'm pleased too. It's to your credit as well as everyone's."

"Yeah," Barbara said with a smile, "I did know when to keep quiet this time."

Using Conflict at Heart Tech

After first avoiding the conflict about Richard, Barbara and Les were able to make it productive. Working with Les, Barbara had come to trust him and indicated that she wanted to discuss the problem openly. Joe helped them see that Richard and the sales reps had important information and insights that were needed to successfully confront the conflict. Les facilitated the open discussion of opposing views so that the group could solve the underlying problem. Together they explored the underlying problem and persisted to reach mutually useful solutions. Conflict was very much a part of the solution to the problem faced by Heart Tech. It was through conflict that the issues were clarified and the solutions developed.

Yet conflict, or rather the ineffective handling of it, was very much a part of the problem in another way, too. At the earlier meeting with Les and Barbara, Joe had simply agreed to Barbara's solution to hire someone like Richard to cope with the threat of litigation, and there had been no contrary views that could have helped them appreciate future difficulties of their decision. The decision was made under the illusion that they had carefully considered the problem from all sides, although they had in fact little understanding of the implications of their decision. Fortunately, through a confrontation of the conflict, they were able to correct their decision before much damage had been wrought.

The new arrangement between Richard and the sales reps will not be effective if conflict continues to be avoided. In fact, Richard's new role has the potential for conflict. The sales reps and Richard will likely disagree now and then about whether a particular client has the expertise needed to use Heart Tech's products. But the new arrangement makes it easier for them to believe they are working together cooperatively and that they want to work for win-win solutions. Then they are more prepared to make their conflicts productive.

Conflict promotes learning and innovation. Barbara and Joe realized the limitations in how they had established Richard's role. They failed to invite representatives from marketing to solicit opposing views and ideas. As it turned out, the check on the sales reps that Richard represented was more costly than they had imagined. Barbara developed the idea and then used her abilities to sell it to Joe, who had neither the inclination nor the background to question her solution carefully. Eventually, they recognized that an open discussion of opposing views, not persuasion, would be much more constructive. They also understood that a solution which makes sense from their standpoint does not mean that it will work for others. Barbara realized that participative management fosters conflict and that these disagreements must be handled well.

Richard, John, Roger, and others at Heart Tech need to be open and skillful to discuss the conflict successfully. However, conflict does not require extraordinary abilities. Because we must all cope with conflict daily, we have learned to handle it. Most likely, you discuss some conflicts with some people well. But you can get better. You can build upon your skills to handle more conflicts, even difficult ones, effectively. The following chapters show how to manage a variety of conflicts productively.

SECTION II
MAKING CONFLICT
PRODUCTIVE

Chapter 5
Conflict Between Colleagues

Marian Batalden saw red when she found Alex Lowe's scribbled note on her desk. "He's done it again," she said to herself. "Alex's always throwing notes at me, telling me to do this or that. I can't read the damn things in the first place...He can't take a minute to write the note properly, but he expects me to take a half an hour to decipher it. Why does he have to leave notes?"

Marian walked over to Joyce Wills. "Remember how I complained about Alex's lousy notes? Well, he's done it again. It seems like such a small thing, but it really burns me up."

"I probably wouldn't like it much either," Joyce said sympathetically. "Why don't you talk to him about it? Maybe he doesn't know how much it bothers you. That would be in the spirit of the retreat we had on the department's values and mission. We're supposed to communicate and work together as a team."

"I should talk to him, I guess. But I don't know. He's apt to take it wrong and get very defensive. He's not the easiest person to talk to."

"True, but you can handle that," Joyce pressed her point. "Just stick to the issue and not let yourself be side-tracked. That's what I've found you need to do with Alex."

"Good advice," Marian said. "I suppose I could also use what I've picked up from the marriage enrichment course Bob and I are taking at church." She settled down to work at her desk, determined to talk to Alex when he got back to the office. If we're to work together, the air needs to be cleared, she said to herself.

Marian felt her stomach and chest tighten when Alex finally returned. She really didn't relish the idea of a confrontation, but she was determined not to let nervousness stop her.

She asked Alex to step into her office for a few moments. "I've been meaning to speak to you about a problem. Do you have a few minutes to talk about it? At the department's retreat, we talked about how we need to work together and cooperate. I'm hoping that we can solve this problem to both our satisfaction, so that it will be better for both of us. "

Alex didn't want to talk about problems with Marian, but he could see no easy way to extricate himself. "Sure, go ahead," he said.

"It's about these notes you put on my desk," Marian said, waving toward the pile on her desk. "They really bother me."

Alex rolled his eyes: So that's what this is all about. It seemed awfully petty to him. "Sorry about that," he said, "I just don't know where to put them. I try to put them in the middle of the desk so you will be sure to see them." He told himself to stay calm. He wanted to end this thing quickly.

"It's not so much where they are. Alex, I can't read them. It takes me forever to read the things. If you could only write a little neater..." Marian was clearly irritated.

Alex began to lose his cool—he wondered what Marian had against him. "Come on, my handwriting is not the best, but it's not that bad either. Don't make a mountain out of a molehill, Marian."

"OK, it's not an earth-shaking issue, I grant. But it's a real pain to read these notes. It's like you think your time is so valuable you can't take a minute to write it properly or talk to me and make sure I know what you want, but I have all day to read your scribbles. And everything always has to be done right away. If you think they are so important, why don't you do them yourself."

"Marian, what's gotten into you? You're little Ms. Cheerful to most people, and now you dump all this on me. Why me?"

"I'm not dumping on you, I'm telling you why I'm upset. I'm not trying to get your goat or win a debate, but to solve our problems so we are both better off." Marian was forceful but did not want to be nasty or self-righteous. She was determined not to get sidetracked by getting into a squabble about being called Ms. Cheerful. Yet she began to realize that she had more on her mind than notes. "Look, it's not just the notes, it's your attitude toward me—towards working with me—that bother me."

"My 'attitude', what's that suppose to mean? I guess you want me to go around smiling all day long. Sorry, that's not me. Maybe you can pretend to be happy all day, I can't."

"I don't pretend to be happy all day. I guess I'm just good natured...I recommend it to you, by the way." Marian wanted to let him know she didn't like being mocked, but she also knew that she did not want to get into a fight on cheerfulness.

"Life's not that happy," Alex said sarcastically.

Marian looked down at her desk for a moment, giving herself some time to calm down and collect her thoughts. This wasn't going the way she had hoped it would. She tried to go back to what she thought was the major problem, Alex's attitude. "I've tried hard to help you ever since you were first hired, but you've been ungrateful. I spent your first month on the job filling you in, showing you the ropes. You never did thank me. We're supposed to work as a team and communicate, but we don't much, do we? You just go on doing your thing. You don't let us know what you're doing and why; you're wrapped up into your own world."

"Of course, you're the great team player. To you, working here for Heart Tech is enough. You're a lifer, I'm not." Alex felt attacked, and defended himself by counter-attacking.

Marian struggled not to take offence at Alex's sarcasm. It suddenly struck her that his attacks on her were really indirect ways to communicate his feelings. He apparently had strong negative feelings toward teamwork, and reservations about Heart Tech.

"I want more than this," Alex continued, waving his hand in the direction of the other offices . "To get it I must really establish myself and know my stuff, not be a weak team player who relies on everyone else."

Marian and Alex elaborated on these issues for what to them seemed like a few minutes, but was nearly half an hour. Marian worked to keep the discussion on feelings and the problems they had between them. She did not let Alex's attempts at humor or mockery push her button and get her upset. She didn't want to become angry and self-righteous about his style of debating. She kept expressing her own feelings and listening carefully to Alex.

"I honestly didn't realize that we both had such strong feelings," Marian said reflectively. "I think we've come to the point of diminishing returns talking like this. We're repeating ourselves. Let's see if we can list the major issues." In the heat of the conflict, Marian had forgotten to use her listening skills, but she now saw an opportunity. She wanted to communicate to Alex that she had been listening to him, understood his feelings and views, and could talk about them without strong criticism or evaluation.

"I want to list as many of your issues as I can," she said. "Perhaps the biggest one for you is that you don't like what I view as helping you. You think I'm just showing off and don't really mean to help."

"That's the general idea. It's like you're just letting me know that you know more than I do."

"The second issue is that you're not sure about this teamwork business. You see being a team player as weak."

"Right. I want to be my own boss, or at least be part of the top group of a dynamic, growing company. I want to prove that I've got what it takes."

"A third issue is your commitment here at Heart Tech. You don't see yourself as working here for years and years, but may want to become the core part of a new venture."

"That's right. I don't see myself taking retirement here."

Alex reluctantly admitted to himself that he was impressed by Marian's impartial and accurate summary of what he had been saying. Suddenly it no longer seemed that the conflict would go on and on and get nowhere. Marian really seemed like she wanted to do something about the problems, not just complain about him.

"It's my turn, I guess," Alex said. "Wasn't there something about notes?" For the first time, they both smiled. "You want my notes to be more legible. That should be pretty easy to correct."

"It would be nice if I could read them. But I think it's part of a larger problem of not letting me know what you're about. I'd be much more keen about making the calls, or whatever the note said, if I knew what the purpose was and why you wanted me and not yourself to do it. That would also help me decipher the note as well."

"I thought I was supposed to be telling you what you said," Alex said, teasing Marion. "I guess I'm getting the message. The notes are part of the issue of my attitude toward working with you and the others. You don't think I'm enough of a team player."

"That's how it strikes me, anyway. You know, I think our discussion has been quite helpful so far," Marian said. "We're both trying to improve how we work together." She wanted to keep the momentum. "We are getting a better idea of what the problems are, but I would like to know more specifics. What exactly do I do that makes you think I am showing off, trying to show you up?" Marian asked.

Alex thought for a moment. "I really haven't thought about how you give me that impression, you just do. Let me think...One thing is that you try to do things for me even when I don't ask for it. The first few days, I just couldn't believe you were giving me all this information and assistance, and I never once asked for it. That just made me suspicious, and I wondered why you were doing it."

"When I help you and you haven't asked, you sometimes aren't sure that my motives are altruistic. Is that what you mean?" Marian again found a good opportunity to use her listening skills.

"That's right, it's like you are doing it for you, not for me."

"I never dreamt that you would take it that way," Marian said. "I assumed that you'd welcome my help but were too shy to ask. I guess giving help can be taken as showing someone up, not helping."

Marian continued. "Let's talk about this teamwork

issue. It'd help if you'd let the rest of us know what you're doing and were more friendly and positive. I'm not saying that you're an awful person, but you come across harsh without any apparent reason."

"I guess I'm always pushing myself. Never satisfied, that's me. I always want to do better." He paused and looked at her intently for a moment. Marian could see he was debating with himself about whether to trust her. "Look," he finally said, "Just between the two of us, I just don't think that my life is here at Heart Tech. I think you've got to be part of the inner circle of a new company to make it big."

Marian translated Alex's comments, hoping to clarify for both of them what he had been saying. "I appreciate your confidence. You seem to be saying that you put a lot of pressure on yourself to do well by yourself and for yourself, and you just don't see where teamwork and friendliness are that important for you."

"That's about it. It may sound cold, but I think it's realistic in this competitive world."

"But is it realistic, Alex? You've got to work with people regardless of where you are. Don't you think Barbara has to deal with people and be a team player? She's got Joe, Les, Al... all those people. Then she has you, me, and everyone here as well, and people in the other departments. Even if you were the head of your own company, you'd have lots of people to work with: Investors, banks, suppliers, customers, and on and on."

"That's a long list, true, but first you must prove yourself."

"But how do you that? You learn a lot through talking and working with other people. I mean really a lot. Plus you have to prove yourself to others. If you get a bad reputation around here, that will follow you. You know this world is sometimes very small; everyone in the industry knows someone who knows you."

"But I don't want to go around smiling and agreeing with everyone."

"No one's asking you to do that. Be your own person, but cultivate others. They'll help you and you'll enjoy them and yourself a lot more. Don't just leave notes asking others to do things. Be willing to help them. Believe me on this anyway, if nothing else."

"You're convincing, Marian, but I'm not quite convinced. I thought you'd be shocked that I didn't want to stay at Heart Tech forever."

"No, I don't expect everyone to want to stay. You never know, things change fast, and someday I may want to leave. If you have a better opportunity elsewhere, go for it. No one wants to hold you back."

They continued to discuss their conflict for some time. They agreed to keep the communication lines open and talk again.

Reflecting on Marian and Alex's Conflict

Marian and Alex made good use of their conflict. They confronted their frustrations and dug into the issues to understand each other better. They began to develop more useful ways to work together.

Through a full discussion of their views, Marian and Alex understood why scribbled notes upset Marian. It took the give and take of the conflict for them to realize that her anger was based on conclusions she had made about Alex. Marian first argued that she was angry because of Alex's attitude. Listening to Alex's questions and comments, she realized that she thought Alex appeared ungrateful and self-centered. If Marian had just complained about notes to Alex and demanded neat notes without further discussion, they may not have understood why the notes bothered her—or what was really going on between the two of them. Alex might have resigned himself to adjusting to Marian's unreasonable need for very neat memos, and would have another reason to think of working elsewhere.

They also came to understand how their opposing views of Marian's assistance had created barriers. Marian felt she was being a helpful colleague by freely giving information and assistance. She thought Alex was a spoiled brat who expected others, perhaps especially women, to wait on him without thought of reciprocating. She found him unpredictable and unreliable. Why didn't he react logically and simply to her help with thanks?

Alex was not irrational. He only suspected that she was trying to demonstrate her superior knowledge. Thinking that she was competing against him, not cooperating with him, he did not feel grateful.

The two of them came to realize that arguing over whose interpretations were right and wrong would not be useful. Once Marian understood Alex's reactions, she could try to convince him that she was not trying to show him up. She can change her actions, perhaps by giving help when he asked for it, and by telling him her intentions directly.

Alex also learned from the conflict. He came face to face with the problems his style of working had created: He thought he could avoid conflict and problems by just doing his own thing. Yet here was Marian, angry and upset with him for being independent and self-centered. He began to realize that doing it alone does not work well in an organization. Marian and other colleagues want to know his plans, aspirations, and obstacles. Then they can share in his work and life and be able to give assistance if needed.

He learned too that his "grumpiness" also disturbed his colleagues. At first they worried that they had done something to make him unhappy; later they decided that Alex was just a negative, egotistical person, and regretted that they didn't have a better colleague. Alex was learning in a concrete way that colleagues depend upon each other, and they need to take each other's perspective and work together.

Marian and Alex both felt more confident after the conflict. They now felt they were in charge of their problems; they controlled their conflict, the conflict did not control them. Without conflict, they would have felt burdened by their frustrations and anger and concluded that they must just learn to live with these feelings. Through the conflict, they expressed their frustrations and anger, and became more aware of their feelings and the reasons behind them. They then used this knowledge to solve problems and improve the way they worked to gether.

Making the Conflict Productive

Marian and Alex worked to make their conflict productive. Although they both had strong feelings—and even a fair amount of anger—they confronted their differences, and took risks to let each other know what they thought and felt. Bolstered by what she perceived to be the values of the department, Marian was determined to dig into the conflict. Originally reluctant, Alex got caught up in the give and take of the conflict. It was not easy, and neither of them would suggest that it was entirely painless, but it worked. They did not close off the discussion prematurely by finding a solution without first letting themselves present their positions fully. Note that they presented both their feelings and the reasoning behind them. Conflict engages both the heart and mind, and requires an openness with feelings and thinking.

Open expression of views must be done skillfully. Otherwise the conflict may escalate and add rather than solve problems. Marian recognized that conflict is a mutual affair—that it takes two to have a conflict and it takes two to manage conflict—and she made this clear to Alex so that he would recognize that they shared a mutual objective. She avoided trying to win the argument or prove she was right and he wrong. Instead, she showed an interest in his feelings and a desire to make the conflict beneficial to him as well.

There was give and take during the conflict. Neither of them attempted to dominate the discussion and get the other to accept their position. If Marian had been the boss, she might have thought that she didn't have to bother listening to Alex's position; she would order neat memos and that would be the end of it. But they were peers, and neither Marian nor Alex could easily make the other accept their solution.

By the same token, Marian and Alex did not rigidly assume that the conflict was a competitive fight. Many people automatically associate conflict with a win-lose fight; once in conflict they fight to win. This expectation is often self-fulfilling, for such fighting usually provokes others to fight to win, too. But because they were willing to be flexible, Marian and Alex were not caught into such a cycle. They realized that their conflict was not a debate to win, but an opportunity to make their work more productive and their relationship more enhancing. They made their own choices rather than blindly assuming they needed to win.

Listening skills were also important to make the conflict productive. Marian demonstrated that she listened carefully, put herself in Alex's shoes, took his perspective, and understood his basic position. She was not so rigid that she could only see the problem from her vantage point, but accepted the challenge of the conflict to see through Alex's eyes. Her listening not only helped her understand, but it reduced Alex's suspicions and made him more willing himself to listen carefully to her views. They were both reassured the conflict was constructive; it was not just sparks flying haphazardly.

By sticking to the major issues and problems, they were able to discuss their opposing views openly without feeling insulted and getting derailed into side issues. It is tempting to become angry and self-righteous when someone has just clearly behaved improperly. However, although Alex made sarcastic remarks, Marian did not rise to the bait. She had evidence that she could have used to show that he was nasty and insulting, but she knew that being self-righteous would have sidetracked them from the major issues, and could well have conveyed that she was trying to prove she was superior after all.

Marion's motivation and skills helped overcome Alex's reluctance. She initiated the discussion, refused to get sidetracked, and finally demonstrated to Alex that she wanted him to benefit and participate in the conflict, not just be a target of criticism. She made sure that Alex understood she wanted to solve the conflict for the benefit of both of them, she demonstrated that she was listening and had understood what he had been saying, and she did not let her button be pushed. But Marian was successful through Alex and needed Alex to be forthright in his opinions and willing to work for mutually useful solutions. Marian did not manage the conflict herself; their success was a joint one.

Chapter 6
Conflict Between Boss and Subordinate

"I've got a problem," Tom Nelson, Al's assistant manager in production, was talking to Glen Southerland, a friend from marketing. "Al just put me in charge of developing an incentive program for the department. He says he wants to reward the hard workers and identify the slackers. I think it's just going to raise a hell of a racket. The operators will first laugh and then they'll threaten to unionize. Between you and me, I'm fed up with trying to live with his half-baked ideas."

"He's not talking that up again, is he? Some people never quit," Glen said, laughing sympathetically.

Tom didn't laugh. "Funny for you, trouble for me," he said.

"Why don't you just go to him and tell him candidly that you think the incentives will be bad for the department?" Glen asked.

"Are you kidding? He'll hold it against me forever.

I wish I had a boss that I could talk with that openly. He talks about teamwork, but he ain't open."

"I didn't realize that things were so strained between the two of you."

"Al's become completely unreasonable. Last year, when we worked on the reorganization, we really clicked. But the atmosphere has changed 180 degrees. I think he's jealous that I'm young and on the way up."

"That doesn't sound like Al to me. He's not the envious type. Anyway, he's too old to worry about future promotions. Look, if the two of you worked so well before, maybe something you said or did got him upset."

"I've been doing my job just fine," Tom said trying to sound confident. "Al's getting hardening of the arteries or something."

"I don't want to take sides in this, but it's not like Al to get upset for no reason. Has he said anything to you that might help us know why he's upset?"

"He gave me decent ratings at my last performance appraisal meeting, but the session was tense. He's nagged me a few times about neglecting the projects he saw as high priority in favor of projects others think are important. But that shouldn't upset him."

"That would bother a lot of bosses. Les would be angry if I didn't work on the tasks he thought were high priority."

"But Al's out of line here. Of course, I take his instructions seriously. But there are other people in the department, too, you know, not just him."

"Maybe Al thinks you're ignoring him. Bosses expect their priorities to be followed, and will usually feel slapped in the face if you don't. You must convince them why other things are more important."

"But he's wrong, I do consider his priorities."

Glen was getting annoyed, not so much at Tom, but at what Tom was risking by being intransigent. He knew that Tom's failure to recognize the need to respond to Al's concerns would cost him a great deal. "Whether he's right or wrong is another issue. It's what he thinks is true that counts. You've got to take your boss seriously. He can make your life miserable. Face the facts, Tom."

Tom had hoped that Al would eventually recognize he was at fault, but now, talking with Glen, he realized the problem wasn't only Al's. "Yeah, I guess you're right. It sounds like I need to take his complaint seriously."

Tom and Glen discussed how Tom might approach the problem. Glen wanted Tom to take the initiative. Al had other pressing issues and concerns and would probably see it as Tom's problem to be solved by Tom.

The more Tom thought about his plan the more he liked it. True, he thought he was wronged, and he certainly didn't like Al's being angry with him. But he was relieved that he could do something about improving the situation. As it was, he felt vulnerable and powerless, and the tension was wearing him out. Confident he was on a good track now, Tom asked to meet with Al to discuss special projects.

Al had mixed feelings as the late afternoon meeting time approached. He wanted the meeting to be short. He still had to meet with Joe to go over the monthly reports. Tonight was his granddaughter's birthday party, and he was not going to be late for that. He was glad Tom wanted to talk; perhaps what he had told Tom before had finally sunk in. But he worried that the meeting would disappoint him.

Tom got down to business quickly. "We seem to have few troubles with the daily work, but we do have some with special projects. Would you agree with that?" Al nodded. Tom continued. "I've been thinking about what you said about taking your priorities on these projects more seriously. I have a proposal that I wanted to run by you that might help both of us understand where we are."

"That would be good, if it worked." Al was trying to sound hopeful, but his irritation with Tom showed.

"I think we should meet regularly, say Monday afternoon for a short while, where we talk just about these special projects." Tom kept to his plan. "We could go over which projects you think are the most important. I could also keep track of the projects from previous meetings and give you short progress reports. It wouldn't have to be elaborate at all."

"A short meeting makes sense."

"We can talk about the problems with the projects as they come up. I can tell you about the demands on my time and perhaps we can reach some consensus about where I should put my efforts."

"That's a good idea. But meeting every week seems too often. How about every other week?" Al felt relieved. Tom's working on low priority projects rather than the ones he wanted bothered him and had started to sour his whole attitude toward Tom. Al didn't like feeling negative toward someone who was supposed to be his right-hand man. But lately, every time he saw Tom, he was reminded that Tom deliberately sabotaged his wishes. Perhaps this was the beginning of the end of this thorn in his side.

His secretary stuck her head in the office to remind Al he was supposed to meet with Joe in ten minutes. "We'll have to continue this another time, I'm afraid," he said to Tom. "But I'm glad we've begun to tackle this problem. I think your idea is a good one."

For the next two months, Tom worked to make the meetings both efficient and pleasant, and did not complain when Al had to cancel one at the last minute. He made it clear that he appreciated Al's taking the time to improve communication and showed he followed through on Al's priorities.

Tom was pleased with his program, but he worried that the potentially explosive issue of incentives was moving closer to the top of the priority list. His preliminary research had only reinforced his objections to incentives. Clearly, pretending to agree with Al was not practical or desirable—Glen agreed with him on that point-but now that he and Al were talking openly, he was on much better ground: he could discuss his objections to the incentive program and get a fair hearing. Tom and Glen talked about how Tom might voice his reservations about the incentives plan in a way Al would find constructive.

At his next regular meeting with Al, however, Tom departed from his plan when he brought up the incentives issues. "I've begun preliminary work on the incentive scheme. I've talked to some people at Aero who have been experimenting with various plans for a year and I've done some reading. Frankly, I just can't see an incentive program. It will just cost us and won't produce."

Al was taken back. ""I think we should try. I think it might do a whole lot of good here."

"It won't work; it'll just get the workers upset."

Al's anger flared. "I didn't hire you to tell me my ideas are wrong, or to be so concerned with employee feelings. We're supposed to run a production department, not be social workers for a love boat."

"But what if they unionize..."

"That's old scare talk. Come on, Tom, I thought you were trying to work with me on this."

Tom felt the urge to fight back, but he realized that would not get him where he wanted to go. He wanted to get back to his original plan. "I don't mean that your idea is wrong. Let's just say that my first impressions about an incentive program are not too optimistic, OK? I may be wrong, who knows? That's why we're doing this preliminary work, right?"

"That's not how it sounded. I've worked a long time in this department, and I'm the head of it. And I say we should have an incentive plan."

"Of course, if you want an incentive plan, we'll have one," Tom said, hoping to sound conciliatory. He didn't like being bullied around, but the fact was that Al did have the final say in the matter. "I have no problem with that. I didn't mean to imply anything else."

"You did sound that way, but go on."

Tom was determined to keep his cool. He did not want to antagonize Al further. He wanted to address the incentive program and show Al that he was taking the idea seriously. "An incentive program can work. How well it can work for us is the question. Even more, it is what kind of incentive program can work for us."

"If you're saying that you are not sure what kind to have, I agree, I'm not sure about the specifics myself."

"You'll be happy, or perhaps relieved, to know that I've completed some preliminary work." Al didn't smile, but his expression softened. "I called a prof I know for suggested readings. What I propose, if it's OK with you, is to give you some of the more informative articles, and maybe my notes on other readings and conversations. Also, I'd like us to have lunch with my friends from Aero Electronics; they've had an incentive program for over a year. I think it would be good if we both started from the same point on incentives and worked together on a program."

"I believe in incentive schemes, but I do admit I don't have a good grasp of exactly how it would work for us. I'd like to talk to those people and do some reading. Could you give me what you think are the most relevant readings?"

"Sure, no problem." Tom then asked, "So you're satisfied with our approach to researching the incentive plans?"

"Yes. I've always wanted to learn more about them, and now I have a way."

In their next meetings, Tom worked to show that he took Al's ideas seriously. He included favorable as well as unfavorable articles about incentive plans, and pointed out both their possible benefits and costs. Offering to set up small pilot projects to test various incentive plans, he explained that the question was what would be useful and practical for the production department, not whether incentive plans are or are not a good thing in general, or which of them was originally right.

Although Tom and Al had sharp differences when they started talking about the specific case of their own department, their discussions now put them in much greater agreement. Their study further reduced their differences as they became aware of the practical complexities of setting up incentive plans. At the end, they decided to rule out incentive plans for individuals as too cumbersome and unproven. Instead, they opted to establish modest incentives for the groups in the department. For example, groups that met their monthly quota would be taken out to lunch at a local restaurant. Tom and Al were pleased they had learned about incentive programs, developed a practical one for their department, and had demonstrated they could work together even when they had opposing views.

Reflecting on the Conflict with the Boss

Tom managed his conflicts both with Glen and Al productively, although there were periods when anger and frustration threatened to derail his efforts at resolving their disputes. Indeed, his conflict with Glen helped him prepare to discuss incentives with Al. Glen challenged Tom's conclusion that the problem was Al's jealousy. He argued that Tom must take the initiative to solve the problem. Once Tom realized that he had contributed to his predicament himself and needed to work to get out of it, he stopped blaming Al, choosing instead to talk with Glen about how to manage his conflict with Al.

Tom's conversation with Glen, a friend and colleague, was unthreatening and open; they could be more spontaneous in expressing their feelings, confident that the warm relationship they had long enjoyed would prevent any lasting ill effects. In contrast, Tom carefully planned for his discussions with Al. He thought that Al would not be open to disagreement and that he had to be more circumspect in approaching Al.

Why was it difficult for Tom to manage his conflict with Al? It is tempting to say: 'Because Al is his boss.' But this answer doesn't take us very far. After all, there are good bosses and bad bosses (the same thing can be said of subordinates), warm boss-subordinate relationships and distant, formal ones. However, the real issue is this: You can't have a relationship that involves only one person. When two or more individuals interact, there will always be some degree of difference between perspectives, experiences, expectations, goals and personalities. If conflict is to be successfully managed, these differences must be taken into account.

Al's attitudes and expectations, for example, made it necessary that Tom be more skilled and deliberate in managing the conflict. Al became easily irritated when his legitimate instructions were ignored, and thought Tom should work hard to correct the mistakes Al identified.

Like most bosses, Al expected subordinates to be responsive. He saw Tom as his assistant who should work with him for the good of the department. He did not want to be unnecessarily burdened by subordinates; he was an important, busy person. He was the manager because of his experience, wisdom, and competence. He also had to take care of demands from other subordinates, colleagues, suppliers, customers, and his own boss. Although he did not like throwing his weight around, Al was well aware that his position was backed with power. As one boss told her subordinates, "If we are to compete, you will lose because one of us will have to go, and I'm staying." In a crunch, he would prevail; if someone was going to be in control, it would be him.

Al did not expect Tom to be submissive, however.

In fact, he would vehemently deny that he wanted to surround himself with "yes men." He saw himself as a strong person capable of handling disagreement. However, he wanted conflicts with subordinates to be handled respectfully and efficiently. The conflict must clearly help him do his important, difficult job of running the department. Colleagues want to handle their conflicts well, but bosses are less willing to be burdened by their subordinates and expect them to work hard to solve problems and manage conflicts.

Tom's attitudes also contributed to making the conflict difficult to handle. Al's criticism and anger upset Tom a great deal. He felt unjustly attacked, but had no good way to right the wrong or force Al to do anything. Tom felt vulnerable; Al had the power to upset his career plans and to make his daily work life miserable. His strong feelings interfered with his thinking. He unrealistically wanted Al to share his point of view and admit he was wrong. Tom prematurely concluded that he was trapped and had no good options.

Fortunately, Tom turned to Glen for help in dealing with his conflict with Al. At Glen's recommendation, Tom worked hard to build a good foundation by demonstrating that he was working with Al for the good of the department and was working on the projects Al thought were important. With this as a basis, it was less likely that Al would view opposition to his incentive plans as simply another example of Tom working against him.

For the most part, Tom was able to show that he shared a common objective with Al, respectfully considered Al's ideas on incentives, avoided challenging his position or authority, demonstrated open-mindedness, and helped Al make good use of the conflict to learn and develop a useful solution. In order to avoid ideological debates that would accentuate their differences without moving them closer to a realistic solution, Tom focused the discussion on a program good for the department. He made their discussions productive and convenient for Al to underline that he was working with Al for the good of the department.

Although conflicts between bosses and subordinates can be particularly difficult to handle, given that they don't enjoy the same amount of power in the organization or over each others' lives, the principles governing their management are really no different from any other conflict. Both parties should try to make the conflict mutually advantageous and promote common interests. All people want to be listened to and have their views respected. They want to be assured that the conflict will help them get their jobs done and will enhance, not harm, their reputation and relationships. But conflicting with a boss requires added sensitivity and persistence, for bosses traditionally expect their subordinates to be responsive and accommodating.

Naturally, most of us would prefer to work for bosses with whom we can talk with freely and who can manage conflict openly. However, this expectation is not always met in the real world: Not all bosses are approachable and open to perspectives or opinions that challenge their own. The subordinate must therefore be willing to work hard to build the kind of foundation that is needed before a conflict can be resolved. Thoughtful planning and preparation become invaluable in this context, particularly if it is the subordinate who has called the meeting to address the conflict in the first place.

And along with this planning must come honesty: It is difficult enough to know our own motivations, let alone someone else's. Is the issue at stake a particular approach to a business problem, your boss's style, or something else? When a new boss is brought on board from outside the company, for example, or is promoted from within, it is not at all uncommon for there to be a struggle for power, or even mistrust, envy, or resentment among the subordinates who predate him or her. In these circumstances, what feels like a disagreement over business procedures is often a clash between egos or a reluctance to adapt to new demands, new ways of doing things. If you can be truthful with yourself about what you're after, you'll be better able to understand what approach you should take in your attempt to resolve a dispute.

Chapter 7
Mediating Conflict

Managers at Heart Tech, like managers in every organization, get involved in other people's conflicts. Such situations require special skills in conflict management. In the last chapter, we saw how Glen listened to Tom's frustrations with Al, and advised him on how he might handle this conflict. He was not in a position to actively mediate their dispute, but he could serve as a disinterested outside party who could be more objective in evaluating what was going on. Because he was not personally involved, Glen was in a better position to see the real issues. Similarly, at the management meetings Joe listened to disagreements between the vice-presidents and tried to make their discussions productive.

The key to managing employee conflicts, as with managing one's own, lies in the ability to choose the appropriate approach and carry it out successfully. Conflicts are too varied for one approach to be always effective. Managers have many options when their employees are in conflict. They can listen, give advice, avoid getting involved, tell them to solve their own problems, or impose a settlement. Unfortunately, many managers are trapped into predetermined ways to respond to employee conflicts.

A traditionally popular approach is to tell the warring employees to knock it off. The manager wants no more bickering, complaining, and gossiping, and threatens to punish-perhaps even fire-the "guilty" parties. A more progressive version of this approach is to understand the conflict, develop a solution, and then impose it upon employees. Many managers assume that their role is to end all disputes: that they must seek out all the facts, determine who is right and who is wrong, and make and enforce a decision.

Imposing a solution and warning employees that they better stop bickering works in some situations. There is some satisfaction to be found in exerting leadership through decisive action, and ending the conflict efficiently. Yet the shortcomings of this approach are not well appreciated. Despite exhaustive work, the manager may be unable to understand the situation fully or create a useful solution. Sometimes, as we saw with Alex and Marion, the apparent source of conflict is not the real problem. Imposing the solution is even more difficult. Employees often believe that the solution is biased against them and the manager has treated them unfairly. They remain angry toward each other, but are now angry with the boss, too.

Mediation is used much less frequently than it should be. A manager mediates by helping employees manage their conflicts themselves. He encourages employees to use good conflict procedures and skills. They must discuss their ideas and feelings openly, emphasize their common goals, demonstrate interest and respect for each other, and seek resolutions that are mutually beneficial. The mediating manager is thus referee and resource person rather than judge and arbitrator.

In addition to avoiding the pitfalls that imposed settlements often generate, skillful mediation yields the benefits of productive conflict. Frustrations are expressed and reduced, problems are understood, the best ideas of several persons are put together to create solutions, the protagonists accept and implement the solution, and feel better about themselves and their work relationship. The manager is satisfied that he has helped his employees solve their own problem and become more skillful. He will be less burdened with future conflicts, for the employees will be able to handle them independently. Moreover, these employees are learning skills and developing ways of approaching problems that will be useful to them as they move into management themselves.

But mediation requires managers and employees to be skillful and patient. This chapter shows mediation at work. Gary Eckberg is confronted with a conflict between Gloria Swanson and Frank Holmes, both of whom work in his department. Gary comes to understand how mediation can be useful in dealing with this problem and he experiments with it to help resolve a long standing conflict.

Gary as Mediator

"You're the one who wants everyone to work as a team, right? Well, I have the evidence that I was right after all," Gary Eckberg said teasingly when he saw Joe in the coffee room.

"No...No...I'm the boss, that makes me right and you wrong," Joe teased back.

"But I have the evidence. Gloria Swanson and Frank Holmes absolutely and in no way can ever work as a team. They can't work in the same office, perhaps not in the same company, perhaps not in the same city. Put them on a task force, they bicker. Ask them to interview applicants, they come running to me complaining that the other said this and that. It drives me bananas."

"They are working together...to drive you nuts." Joe couldn't resist saying. Then he became more serious. "What do they do?"

"I didn't mean to drag you into this, but it's a real

headache for me. It's little things and it's big things. Gloria will tell me that Frank paints such a rosy picture of the company to new applicants that she's afraid they won't believe they have to work. Frank will tell me that Gloria is so harsh in interviews that our best applicants are turned off. Gloria complains that Frank isn't doing his fair share of the work on the hiring procedures task force; Frank complains that Gloria's work on the task force isn't worth the hassle of having her on it. They blame each other when their report is late. It goes on and on like this."

"Ugh...I didn't realize it was so serious," Joe said. "What sorts of things have you tried?"

"Just about everything I could think of. I've listened to them complain and tried to be sympathetic. I've told them to stop bickering and act like mature adults. I've threatened them. I've stepped in and told them you do this and you do that, and now I don't want to hear any more noise from either of you."

"Nothing's worked, I guess?"

"For a little while things are quiet, at least for me. But I think it just goes underground for a while: They gossip and complain to their friends. It's like they want to divide the office into those who support Gloria and those support Frank. So I'm not left out of it for very long. Soon they start up on some different issue, and we're right back to square one."

"So what do you think is going on?" Joe asked. "Underneath it all, I mean."

"It must be a personality clash that can't be worked out," Gary said. "They don't like each other and they're not going to like each other. I don't see how I or you or whoever can make a difference. I'm thinking of letting one, maybe both go. They're good employees otherwise, but they aren't that good. Especially when they start dragging everyone around them into the dispute. It gets pretty disruptive, you know."

Joe was quiet for a moment as he considered some

alternatives. "I've got an idea, Gary. I read an article on company strategy that talked about how some company couldn't get very far because two department managers were warring with each other. Finally, the CEO sat down with them and told them he wanted them to work out their constant bickering, and he was going to wait until they got to the bottom of the problem and found a way to live with each other. I thought it was pretty impressive. Couldn't something like that work for you?"

"Get them together in the same room and let them hassle each other? It might work. Better they hassle each other than me. Seriously, though, I think they'd be at each other's throats within minutes."

"They're already at each other's throats," Joe reminded him, "but this would give them a chance and reason to talk. You wouldn't get stuck in this game of trying to solve their problems for them, or being blamed for your decisions. You let them know you want them to discuss and resolve their conflict. You can help them, but it's their problem to solve."

As the two of them talked, Gary became less skeptical. Gary decided to take Joe's advice. He broke the news to Gloria and Frank. "It should come to you as no surprise that I've noticed the two of you have had several, even many, differences of opinion, disputes, debates, skirmishes, battles, and clashes. Major wars mercifully broken up with a few periods of truce."

Gloria and Frank smiled slightly. They appreciated Gary's humor. But they were also somewhat nervous about what he was leading up to.

"Unfortunately, this has been like a bad movie that doesn't know when to quit," Gary continued. "It's disrupted the office and upset me. But it probably has been even worse for the two of you." Gary then outlined his plan and they agreed to meet. To Gary's surprise, while they were not cheerful, they did not object.

To begin the meeting, Gary reminded them that their

purpose was to work out their differences. He wanted them to resolve their conflict, and ideally to learn to discuss future difficulties without him. He reminded them to speak to each other, not him, and to let each other speak without interruptions. His job, he said, was not to act as a judge, but to see that they both had the opportunity to express themselves.

He handed out the guidelines for their discussion and talked about them briefly: They must describe what the other does that is frustrating, listen to each other, avoid insults, avoid trying to prove one is right and the other wrong, and work for solutions that help each of them. First they were to get the issues out on the table, and then they would try to find solutions. It was not mandatory that they resolve everything now, but it was important they begin.

Silently Gary went over his own guidelines. Les had warned him that most managers want to be active, but this kind of situation required that he resist the temptation and try to let them talk. The key, Les said, was balance: Show concern for both persons, but don't try to decide who is right and wrong, or appear to be an ally of one against the other.

Gary asked Gloria to begin by expressing her views of the problem. She looked at Frank and started fast. "I think a good part of the problem is that you're too soft. You're so laid back it's as if you were back home on a California beach, not in a company that wants to grow in a demanding market." Gloria continued on this theme for a few minutes.

"If 'soft' is believing in the people at Heart Tech then I plead guilty." Frank was irritated, but he remained controlled. "Soft is better than creating a lot of distrust by being hostile and unapproachable. We're supposed to be a family here, or haven't you paid any attention to our president lately."

Gary held back from warning Frank about personal

attacks. It's better, he thought, to let some momentum build. He could always step in if things threatened to go out of control or get ugly.

"The personnel department must be concerned with hiring people and rewarding them when they get the job done. We need to appear tough-minded if the department is going to be respected in this company." Gloria turned to Gary. "Isn't that right, Gary?"

Gary began to agree, but caught himself. He did not want to be pulled into the discussion so early. Then it hit him. Gloria could have been trying to get him on her side. Instead of agreeing, Gary said, "I don't want to take sides here; I want a resolution. So far, Gloria, you've said you think Frank is soft, and Frank, you've said—or at least implied—that Gloria is hostile. These are mild insults that we probably could nicely do without. Can we get more specific about your differences instead of these general labels?"

Gloria and Frank continued for some time to reveal their impressions and feelings toward each other. Gary paid attention, and helped to summarize their positions. He frequently had to step in to remind them to be specific and avoid even mild insults. Gloria acknowledged that it was good to talk about these things, but she felt they weren't getting anywhere. Gary reassured them that he saw progress being made and they shouldn't leap to solutions prematurely. Somewhat relieved, though not entirely convinced, they continued to talk. Gary knew that as long as they were making progress he did not need to say much.

After an hour and half of discussion, Gary asked Gloria and Frank to summarize their findings and record them. They concluded that they found it easier to talk to others about their difficulties than to each other, and that they both felt a lack of respect for their competence. They admitted, however, that they also felt a great release and wanted to talk again.

"I think it's best if we set a specific time to meet and talk," Gary proposed. "I'd hate to leave it up in the air and have the two of you never get around to serious talking again. We need to keep the ball rolling. I can meet with you again. Or if you prefer, the two of you can meet without me. In which case, send me a short memo which summarizes your findings from each meeting."

After some discussion, Gloria and Frank decided to meet by themselves three more times, and then meet with Gary and talk about their progress and their plans for working together. They agreed that not all problems had been solved, but they had cleared the air and made a beginning. They also agreed they needed to keep working.

Gary was pleased, but he was surprised at how tired he felt. He commented on it to Joe the next day. "Gloria and Frank are making progress. It's not easy to listen so carefully and hold myself back. I didn't realize that I'm so used to talking. Not talking is hard work."

"I know what you mean," Joe said. "I find I have to hold myself back during the management meetings. I like to talk too. I'm glad things went so well."

"Something else I learned. Without knowing it, I've actually been feeding the conflict. When they were fighting, they would come into my office, ask me a question or make a comment, and, if I agreed, would run back and say I supported them. Half the time I didn't even know they were in conflict, much less that they were using me to wage it. I like it much better helping them resolve the conflict than being part of the battle."

Gary was learning important skills to mediate conflict. Realizing that the first rule is not to make the conflict worse, Gary resisted the temptation to impose an arbitrary decision that implied that Gloria or Frank was right and the other wrong. He showed that he was an ally of both and was determined that they reveal their feelings, get the issues out on the table, and listen to each other so that they could develop a mutually acceptable solution.

Chapter 8

Using Conflict to Make Decisions

"I just wanted to let you know that we're meeting and making progress on how Richard and the sales reps work together. They're beginning to work as a team," Barbara said as she knocked at Les's office door. "Thanks again for your help."

"My pleasure. It's good to hear that progress is being made somewhere, because it's not happening here. Joe asked me very specifically to get a more coordinated international marketing program together, but I haven't been able to get it all together. It's so easy to get distracted by immediate concerns. Plus it's hard to figure out what to do. Simon comes in and suggests that we should contract with a technical sales group; Katie suggests that we hire our own people like Manuel down in South America. They all have good reasons. Others are like me, are not sure what we should do. I hate the thought of letting Joe down."

"Joe knows it's difficult, that's why he gave it to you." Barbara tried to be supportive.

Les smiled weakly. "I'd like some progress anyway."

Barbara saw he was still distressed. "You know, an article I just read had an interesting approach to making difficult decisions. Before the company makes any acquisition, it forms two small groups. One takes the side that they should acquire the business and the other takes the position that they not acquire it. The groups do their homework, research, discuss, and present their positions, and then they hash it out from there."

"We did something like that where I worked before," Les said. "We couldn't decide whether we should expand production by remodeling an existing plant or by building a new plant altogether. We had teams research both options, and then a shootout at the end. It's an interesting idea, certainly worth thinking about."

Barbara and Les discussed its pros and cons, and what would be required to make it work. Les decided to try it.

Les reminded his staff of the need to develop a coherent, effective international marketing plan. The company needed to increase sales if it was to continue to develop new products. A major stumbling block was whether to develop their own sales force or contract with an established international marketing agency. He wanted his people to become involved in the decision and had worked out a way for them to participate.

He assigned Simon Chan, Katie Wells, and Dick Andrews to the group that would defend the position that they should develop their own sales force. Mark Boland, Shannon DeVries, and Ray Norberg were given the position that they should contract with a marketing agent. When Simon protested that he should be on the other team because he believed in contracting out, Les explained that he could help the group anticipate opposing arguments. Then they could better develop their own arguments and defend them with the other group.

"I agree with Simon that some changes should be

made," Ray said. "It's not fair that we have the stronger position and also the stronger people."

Everyone laughed. So far, they had listened with the same spirit of friendly competition that they exhibited in the company volleyball games.

"You may think you are stronger now, but wait until we're done with you," challenged Dick.

"They should have a bigger budget just to make it fair," deadpanned Shannon.

"I can see where you guys are going to have a difficult time getting into this," Les broke in. "It makes me proud to be part of the marketing team. Now why do I suddenly wish I hadn't just refinanced my house?" More laughter. "Seriously, I don't want this to be a wild west, cowboy shootout with only one man standing at the end. The point of this is not to outmanuever and win but for all of us to make the best decision we can."

"Aw, you're taking all of the fun out of it," Katie said in mock frustration. More laughter. "Really, Les, I think we all know what you're getting at. We're only kidding...I think."

"Sure, you're kidding," Les could tease, too. "We'll just plan to have an ambulance on hand for the casualties."

Les explained the general procedure. The groups had ten days to prepare. They should discuss the issues, read, interview people from possible marketing agents, and in other ways develop the arguments, facts, and reasoning to support their position. Then they would meet the other group and Les and Barbara would chair the meeting. Each group would first present its views forcefully and then there would be a general, give-and-take discussion. The purpose of the discussion was to get as many facts and reasons out for both positions, and for everyone to get to know them. Near the end, each group would have to list the major arguments of the other group to make sure they understood each other.

The next day, while the discussion was still fresh and they had time to mull over the arguments, they would try to find a solution. This time they would not argue for their assigned position, but everyone would work together to develop the best solution possible.

"Each group has to argue its position as best it can," Les reminded them. "But please keep in mind that the overriding goal is not for one group to win or impose itself on the other, but for us to dig together into the issues and find a solution that we believe in and can live with. Any questions?"

"Within our groups, we are supposed to provide a united front, right?" Mark asked.

"When we have the first discussion, you all should present your group position as persuasively as possible," Les answered. "But of course you might have lots of disagreement as you prepare and plan for your defense."

"No further questions? OK, then let's begin. Can the two groups meet and get organized? Start thinking about your position and developing your arguments. Map out how you can do necessary research and planning for the shootout—things like when and how you can meet to coordinate your effort."

The groups quickly got down to business. They started to list their arguments, and, with Les's prompting, planned how they would get more evidence for their positions. The "contract sales" group wanted to interview representatives from the two most likely marketing agencies, as well as some people from companies that used these agencies. The "own sales" group planned to interview people who had experience in companies with an international sales force. Les suggested that one person from the other group sit in on these interviews as well. Each group should get information and ideas that supported the other side to help them prepare their own position.

Les had little direct observation of the groups for the ten

days, but he heard favorable reports. They divided up their tasks and stayed late to hammer out their arguments. Les enjoyed the general excitement and involvement. He felt confident that something good was going to come out of all it.

The day of the "big game," as the staff dubbed it, arrived with flair. The "own sales" group passed out "WE CAN DO IT!" buttons, and Simon had a zombrado from Mexico, Katie a Russian fur cap, and Dick a Chinese Mao hat. The "contract sales" group had made a giant poster, "STAY LEAN AND MEAN," and dressed most conservatively.

Les welcomed everyone, and announced, "Believe it or not, this is the beginning of making a serious decision. Let me go over the ground rules. Each group presents its case in half an hour or less. The other group is not to interrupt unless they really don't understand the point. Then we will open the discussion for give-and-take. I don't expect us to make a decision today, but I do expect to know a lot more about the issue."

The groups' presentations were impressive. They had obviously thought both about the content of their arguments and how to make their case convincing. The give-and-take part of the debate was particularly enjoyable. There were humorous moments, and many thoughtful ones. Les periodically reminded them that they best listen because at the end of the discussion they must each write down the other group's arguments. He knew everyone was taking the exercise seriously, but he was also a little worried. At one point, he turned to Barbara and said, "This is exciting, but are we any closer to an answer?"

Barbara smiled and said, "Tomorrow, tomorrow."

After 40 minutes of discussion, Les interrupted. "Perhaps we have gotten out most of the arguments for both sides. Now I want each group to list the arguments and facts the other group used to defend its position. This is to make sure we understand each other."

The groups drew up their lists, and then presented them to each other. Each pointed out when the other group was in error or incomplete. Les collected these lists for distribution, and then Les began to close the meeting, asking Barbara if she had any comments. "I found the discussion both energetic and thoughtful," she said. "It was fun to watch and very informative. It looked like you had fun too."

The others agreed, adding that the session made them think and get involved. Les reminded them that this should be a good foundation for tomorrow's meeting.

The next meeting had no buttons or placards, and the noise level was lower. But the discussion was lively. Although there was no obvious, simple solution, they created one that they believed would work. The solution depended in part on the area of the world. Having some-one like Manuel in South America worked well largely because he knew the culture and he knew Heart Tech. But such a combination probably wasn't possible in the Middle East or China.

They also realized that the decision depended in part on the number of products to be marketed. If new products came on stream, especially state-of-the-art ones, having their own sales force was more practical and desirable. If new product development slowed down, then using a marketing agent made more sense. What they should do then depended upon the company's directions. They listed the market areas where having their own sales force was clearly the choice, those areas that an agent was needed, and those areas that it depended upon finding the right person or the product mix.

Les was satisfied. They had the makings of a successful solution, and its underlying rationale was understood by all. The decision allowed them to be flexibile in respond-ing both to changes and to practical issues such as finding the right staff.

Les asked them to talk about their reactions to how they

made the decision. There was general agreement that the procedure had worked. Mark, however, was worried: "One problem is that it restricts you because you have to argue for only one point of view."

"But you end up arguing whatever position you want, don't you?" Katie countered.

"It seemed to me," Ray said, "that I was freer to speak. We could say whatever we wanted, we could be wild and daring because we were just defending a position."

"That's right," Simon said. "In most meetings, we're so worried that we might be wrong or look unreasonable that we get very conservative. Everyone says the safe thing. Here, you could be more speculative. It can lead to some wild thinking, but some creative thinking as well."

"We felt freer to disagree with each other, too. You don't have the same fears that you're going to make a fool of yourself or step on someone's toes," Shannon said. "First we're suppose to disagree. Plus you know that you're criticizing the other's assigned position, not one that he necessarily has personally embraced. It's easier to disagree without fear that someone would take it personally and get defensive."

Several people said they found it easier to speak up because they had a chance to work out what they were going to say in their small group. Group members spotted weaknesses of fact and logic that made the arguments stronger. At traditional meetings, they were on their own and had to speak cold. It was easy to feel intimidated: You worry about appearing incompetent and risking embarrassment.

Les wanted to know whether anyone had trouble getting motivated because they had no personal reward at stake. On the contrary, they said; they were motivated by defending their views from the attack by the other group. They also had the incentive to look sharp to Les and Barbara. The other group's arguments got them thinking both about the problem in general and about defending their position. They also knew that a better decision would help the company, the department, and them.

Dick observed that he found it difficult to switch gears from defending his group's assigned view to focusing on finding a solution. His mind had been set one way and he had thought of attacking the other group and getting his position adopted. Ray thought that listing the other's arguments and waiting a day helped them focus on developing a good solution, not defending their position.

Several people commented that the decision was much better than what most groups come up with. In so many meetings, the person who is the most prestigious or the most fluent or speaks up at the right time determines the decision. Sometimes no one wants to disagree with the boss or upset an apparently happy consensus by disagreeing. This procedure helped them avoid these problems.

Katie seemed to be speaking for everyone when she said, "The approach really got us involved. It made participation and teamwork a reality, not just a slogan." The procedure, everyone agreed, was good for getting people involved and interested in a problem. However, they did not want to use it all the time. The problem should be important and the solution not apparent. Yes, it was exciting, but it was a lot of work, and they had other things to do.

Afterwards, Les and Barbara met briefly in Les' office and agreed that the meeting was a success. "But you know, Les confided, "through it all I felt a little funny, like I wasn't really doing that much."

"You did a lot. You planned the whole procedure," offered Barbara.

"It almost seemed too easy."

"I've had the same sort of feeling at some of our department meetings lately. What it may be is that we usually do most of the talking, persuading, and dominating, that when we get others really involved we sometimes feel a bit lost."

"I guess I did most of my work in setting the procedure up and overseeing it. I influenced how we made the decision rather than the decision itself."

Controversy in Decision Making

Heart Tech's marketing group used a conflict of ideas to help them explore issues and make sound decisions. They expressed their ideas forcefully, but were also open to understanding other points of view. They dug into the issues to develop a full understanding of a complex problem and incorporate various ideas into a creative, useful solution. Consensus and agreement were reached through direct, open discussion of conflicting opinions.

Harmony has traditionally been much lauded, but research has documented that avoiding controversy undermines decision making. Studies have shown that when managers suppress their differences, they can make poor decisions that threaten the credibility and vitality of the company. They remain ignorant of risks and opportunities, and make decisions without thoughtful analysis. They court disaster as well as stagnation.

Individuals by themselves do not have the motivation and information to challenge their own ideas. But by working together, people can open-mindedly explore, combine ideas, and create solutions. However, once again, the key lies in people knowing that they can express their opposing views openly. In controversy, managers are apt, when confronted with an opposing position, to doubt their own position, ask questions to explore alternatives, take opposing information seriously, develop a more accurate view of the situation, and incorporate opposing positions into their own thinking and decisions. Through conflict, decision makers come to understand opposing positions, develop alternatives, and adopt creative solutions.

But not all conflict of ideas is useful; conflict must be well-managed. Controversy, like other kinds of conflict, needs to be discussed cooperatively. The decision makers must understand that their opposing views do not mean that they have opposing goals and objectives. All the members of Heart Tech marketing wanted the best staffing plan possible for the department; however, they saw different solutions to the problem. They knew that it was not important that their original position be right and accepted, but the department as a whole should be right at the end of the discussion.

It was also critical that they were able to maintain this strong sense of common endeavor through the conflict. Many people are sensitive to disagreement and feel insulted when others argue against them. It is important in controversy to communicate appreciation and acceptance of other people although you disagree with their ideas. Decisions-makers who feel personally threatened are likely to get defensive, counter-attack, assume the conflict is competitive, and fight to prove their idea is right. People who believe others are trying to dominate them are also likely to believe the conflict is competitive. The marketing group was also able to allow everyone a chance to be heard and to influence the solution. Respect and openness contribute to making controversy productive.

Well-managed conflict is critical to successful decision-making. It contributes to the quality of solutions and the excitement of solving problems. Independent thinking, the right to dissent, and forums for discussion help initiate controversy. The key to productive controversy lies in assigning, as Les did, reasonable opposing positions to defend. Then the controversy can be used to work toward a mutually useful solution, one that is created out of the clash of opposing ideas and information.

Chapter 9
Making a Budget

"I hate this time of year," Joe blurted out to Gary as they discussed Gary's budget proposals for next year. "These budgets are a royal pain in the neck."

Gary quickly appreciated Joe's frustrations. "Isn't it wonderful, this getting together as a team and working out a budget? It makes you feel proud to be part of it all."

Joe felt relieved to have said something. He knew that, as CEO, the final decision was his, but he didn't like the adversarial atmosphere that always seemed to permeate discussions of the budget. And frankly, he had nagging doubts that the way they had been coming up with a budget over the past years was flawed in some way. "You have to worry about your own budget," he said, "but I get into every department's. Then I have to convince everyone that my choices are good ones. But the worst of it is that I'm not so sure that when we're all done that we have the best budget."

"If it's any comfort, we did the same sorts of things at CompDatum. Let's be candid...I know you're going to cut us back, and so does everyone else. So what do we do? We ask for the moon, knowing we're going to settle for what we probably really need, right? It's all part of business. I guess this strains your team idea, though, doesn't it?"

Joe agreed that everyone must live with budget hassles. Airing his frustration helped him feel a little less stressed.

However, the next day in his meeting with Al, Joe again felt his frustration mounting. "Al, why do you do this to me? Didn't I ask everyone to come up with a lean, trim budget this year? We're trying to be frugal. You can't call this a highly defensible budget. You have new positions, new equipment, the works. Why not BMW's for the managers, and MagicWagons for the supervisors? Wouldn't that all help production?"

Al liked debate, but not sarcasm. "Come on, Joe, that's bull and you know it. These things we ask for make sense to us. We haven't asked for luxuries, and we don't expect to get everything we ask for."

"But you guys come in here with a wish list, not a budget, and then expect me to say no, no, no all the time."

"That's right. That's what we've been doing."

"But I don't like it."

"I don't like it either," Al said. "In the early years, you told us we weren't visionary enough, that we didn't ask for all those things that would make us a great company. Once we learned that lesson, though, you suddenly wanted us to be more frugal. I know you'll cut us back regardless of how worthy our requests. I can live with that if that's what you want. But now you seem to want to change the rules again."

"OK, OK. Look, I didn't mean to jump on you, Al. Don't take it personally. I'm just getting disillusioned with how we do the budgets."

"I can see why you're frustrated," Al said, accepting

Joe's apology. Once again, he found himself being impressed at how easy Joe made it to say what was on your mind. "I don't think much of this budget process, either. I enjoy the planning and thinking ahead, but negotiating with you and our meetings about the budgets are no fun. It's hard not to feel that you've lost something. Though some departments may feel like winners, most of us feel like losers."

"I don't think there's much we can do about it. We really have to be careful with the budget, and there's just so much money to spend. Sure, when money's tight, some departments will win, and some will lose. That's just business reality, right?"

"But I wonder if it has to be this way," Al said. "There must be a better way of deciding what should be funded."

Joe laughed. "I'm the one that's usually optimistic. But realistically, each department wants more for itself, and they'll fight each other to get it."

"There's something I want more than a sweet budget for the production department and that's a strong company. I think everyone feels the same. If we really understood each other's budget requests, I bet you'd be surprised at how much we could agree on what the company needs and what it doesn't need."

Joe shook his head. "I believe in involvement and participation, too, but it's hard to see how they can work here. Even the meeting we have on the budget is strained."

"But in the budget meeting, we all aim to get the most for our departments. That's what our people want us to do. You even tell us to speak up for our department. We're jockeying for position, not working for the company. Our discussions are so general that we never understand what others really want and why."

"I'd be delighted if we could develop better procedures."

Joe and Al discussed ways to have a more open, successful budget process. Joe felt the adrenaline beginning to flow. He was now convinced that maybe there was a way to have a budget without the padding, games, and acrimony he had assumed were inevitable.

In the budget meetings he later held with the other department heads, Joe talked of his frustrations with present procedures. He was relieved to learn that everyone shared his frustration, But he was surprised at how confident they were that they could develop better procedures.

Joe brought up the budget issue to the management committee. "As you know, I'm not happy with the way we develop the budget. It puts me in a squeeze, and makes me the final arbitrator. I can say "No" and do so in many ways. But I'm not sure we really have the best decisions at the end. Talking with you all has convinced me that there must be a better way."

"And that way is for me to say 'No!' Gary couldn't resist the wisecrack before serious business was to begin.

"Amazingly, Gary's actually right...sort of," Joe deadpanned. "I want us all to say 'No.' But also 'Yes.' It's our company and it's our budget. The budget should reflect what we're trying to do and where we're going. It should be our corporate philosophy made very concrete. We should know what the budget is and what it's supposed to do for us. We'll all live with the consequences."

"I like that," Al said. "I'm not happy with how we do it now. It's too stressful and the results are unsatisfactory even when we do get what we want."

"You seem to get what you want, but do we want it? That is the question," Les joked. "My department doesn't even get what it needs." Gary and Barbara joined in the fun of arguing that their departments always lost out to others.

"We may have begun new budget procedures too late," Joe said laughing. "What I propose is that this group become responsible for the budget. It will be our role to develop the best budget possible for the company. The tricky part is that you must all argue for your own department—if you don't who will? But you must also take the company's perspective as a whole."

"Can we do both, really?" Gary doubted. "Won't we just end up the same place we are now, giving a compromised, wishy-washy position."

"I'm not clear about the specifics," Joe admitted. "But we al agree a change is needed. I'm open to suggestions about how we can actually do it. I was thinking that each one of you would distribute your position beforehand and then argue it here at the meetings. The rest of us would ask questions and you'd have to be prepared to answer them."

"That would intimidate me," Les said. "It's like putting one against five."

"And it would take a long, long time to get through the budgets in any depth," Al added.

"Perhaps some of the work could be done in smaller groups outside the meeting," Barbara suggested. "That might be less intimidating and more efficient."

"Right. We could pair up and one of us could become an expert on another's budget and we could present our views to the person and then the group," Gary proposed. "That way each of us would have some feedback about how others might react to the budget, and then we can change our budget or be prepared to defend them."

"I like that," Les said. "We could switch who we work with from year to year. In a few years we would be experts on the whole company."

"Sounds good, sounds interesting," Joe nodded.

They discussed procedures for some time. They were pleased with the progress they made working together. They decided that two of them would team up with the respective department managers to examine the departments. One of them would take the department's perspective and help the department manager argue his or her case. The other would take the company's perspective. After the three had a chance to talk, they would present their findings to the management team which would ultimately approve budgets.

"I'm excited about our plan," Joe concluded. "I think we'll run into some learning curve problems for a while, but in the long run it should be very useful."

"I like the procedures, too, but I think we should feel free to play with them," Les suggested. "We may want to modify them as we use them."

Conflict and Scarce Resources

Joe and the others on the management team used conflict to forge new, more productive procedures. Through an open discussion of their frustrations, they identified the shortcomings of the way they had been developing the budget. By voicing their various opinions, they created and instituted new procedures. Conflict will also help them use the experience they gain along the way to adapt the procedures. It would be unrealistic to expect they will develop perfect procedures without trial and error. Rather, they will be able to discuss the problems they encounter as they use the new procedures and put together ideas to make them more effective. They are, in short, on their way to managing their differences constructively to develop a budget.

They were successful although the conflict was over scarce resources, a situation that because of its very nature often leads to angry confrontations in organizations: The more funds allocated to one department the fewer funds allocated to another.

Scarce resources underline many win-lose conflicts, but scarce resources do not inevitably result in competitive battles. The managers at Heart Tech at first focused on getting as much funding as possible for their own individual departments. This orientation made the conflict competitive. Knowing they could not be overly aggressive and hostile, the managers were restrained in how they wage the battle—but they still felt pitted against each other. However, they were able to redefine the conflict and problem as one in which their objective was to develop a budget that worked for the company as a whole. They saw this approach as challenging and potentially very rewarding for them and the company. By recasting their budgetary differences in a more "holistic" and cooperative context, they created an environment in which they could work together successfully.

Heart Tech's experience with the budget process will serve them well in other areas as well. For example, such human resource issues as job assignments and promotions can be viewed as scarce resource problems. John Buchan and Roger Cumberland both wanted to be promoted to the position of Les's assistant marketing manager. Since only one could be promoted, they were obliged to make a choice: They could handle the conflict either cooperatively or competitively. If they focused on their competition, they would seek promotion at the expense of other goals and fight aggressively. They might gossip, criticize each other publicly, and pretend to help the other while actually frustrating him.

John and Roger can, however, handle their conflict constructively. While still committed to being promoted, they would recognize other, cooperative goals. They would work together to do their present jobs and enjoy each other's esteem and friendship. They would understand that they will both be better off if they continue to work together.

John and Roger agreed to contain their competition and to continue to work together. They accepted that each would present his best case for promotion, but they agreed to avoid public criticism, help each other do their present jobs, and continue to golf together on weekends.

In this way they strengthened their work relationship and friendship and enjoyed the respect of the department.

Concluding Comments

The Heart Tech management team's conflict over the budget illustrates that conflict is not a given, but that people construct it. People choose how to define a conflict situation and whether it will be seen as a mutual problem or a competitive, win-lose battle. Plentiful resources do not insure a cooperative view of conflict. Colleagues can fight competitively over self-esteem. They assume that if others are successful, then they are less successful. They can battle over social esteem; they assume that if their boss praises a colleague they are less appreciated. Yet there is no pre-determined limit to self and social esteem.

Of course, scarce resources can make resolving conflicts more difficult. At the same time, though, scarce resources make the need for overall mutual dependence more compelling. A financial bankruptcy, periods of economic slowdown, or other crisis may make it very clear to all employees that they must bury narrow interests to work together to save the company and their jobs. If they understand this, they will be able to discuss their opposing views openly to further their common interests.

This is a critical point, one worth repeating: People make choices to define and manage their conflict. Conflict just does not happen; people construct it. When they define it as a cooperative conflict and pursue mutual interests and avoid a win-lose approach, they use their conflict to upgrade their procedures and strengthen the way they work together to get things done.

THE CONFLICT
POSITIVE
ORGANIZATION

Chapter 10
Company Philosophy

"We're getting close to our tenth anniversary, and, I hope, closer to being a team." Joe began the management meeting. "You do remember our 'Team at Ten' goal? I don't want this to be an empty slogan."

"We're making progress; we feel more like a team, don't we?" Al said. Others concurred.

"I agree we're getting there, but it seems to me that something like this is just not achieved and then it's there forever," Les said to the whole group. "We've got to keep building upon it and using it."

"Use it or lose it applies here, as well as other places." Gary was still funny but not as sarcastic.

"I don't want us to pretend everything is wonderful and to sweep problems and frustrations under the rug," Joe said. "I'd like us to brainstorm about the issues and areas that we think need attention in how we manage and are organized... in how we get things done. You've all given me ideas and comments on the things concerning

---

you. Thanks for responding so quickly. Let's see what we've got."

Joe wrote the suggestions of team members on an overhead for everyone to see. He wrote down both major and minor items without comment because he wanted to get the ideas out and see what was on people's minds.

As the team examined the list, Joe looked around at the faces of his managers. He was curious to see how they would respond to such an open-ended challenge. After some general discussion of the list, Barbara pointed out some interesting connections. "Two of the more important items are very related, I think. Les wants to make more specific plans for our marketing staff and needs some decisions about our product offerings. We also think that we have a problem with our budgets because our understanding of the company perspective is still a little vague and uncertain."

"That's right," Les agreed. "We still have to decide where our company is going—our long range goals. By the way, Joe's idea of developing a corporate philosophy fits in with this too."

"We on the team probably have a better idea of where we're going than others," Al said. "I think our discussing the budget has helped us figure out what the company is trying to do. It's the people who report to us that are not so aware. That's one reason our people are disappointed that we haven't stood up for our departments more in the budget meetings. If everyone knew where we're going, they could accept our decisions better."

"I suppose so, but I have to admit I break out in hives when people talk corporate philosophy and culture," Gary said. "Most times they sound like just so many platitudes designed to make executives feel good about themselves. If we're going to do one, we need to make ours concrete and realistic, not just nice sounding words."

The team discussed the need for corporate philosophy and strategy and how specific they should be. "We're

getting some consensus that we want a company philosophy that inspires us as well as describes us," Joe summarized. "There also seems to be agreement that developing
a philosophy has high priority. I suppose this team should
be responsible for it."

"It would be great if we could involve other people,
too," Al responded. "The rest of the organization needs to
know what we're about. After all, they're part of the
family, too."

" I see your point, Al, but there's a logistical problem
here, it seems to me. How can we have everyone at a
meeting?" Joe asked.

"We could break up the philosophy and strategy into
parts, and then have task forces work on them," Les said.
"We could be assigned to different task teams and then
recruit volunteers from the rest of the company."

There was general support for Les's idea, but it was
difficult for the team to decide on their specific assignments. Corporate philosophy should be a coherent statement; dividing it up seemed arbitrary. Nor would it be
good if one team worked to develop a position that was
not compatible with what other task forces were doing.
After some prolonged discussion, they settled on two task
forces. One was to focus on external issues and stakehold-
ers: The customers the company serves, how the company
serves them, and corporate strategy to develop new competitive advantages. The second team would concentrate
on internal matters: The company's management values
and procedures. Each task force was mandated to develop
a position and present it to the management team who in
turn would debate and discuss it. The team would make
the final statement but it promised to consider the task
forces' reports open-mindedly.

Team members would be on the task forces to communicate management's thinking and help the task forces
present their findings to the management team. However,
the team members recognized that they did not want to

dominate. The chairs would be selected from outside the management team. Les and Brian were put on the strategy task force and Al and Barbara on the management one. Gary was asked to coordinate the task forces.

Strategy Task Force

Brian was reluctant to join the strategy task force when Joe asked him. "We already have a strategy: Develop as many state-of-the-art electronic medical devices as we can and then try to sell as many as we can."

"Well, that's been our basic strategy, such as it is, but perhaps it needs to be examined," Joe replied. "We've both favored this kind of growth, but other people have other ideas. Some feel it's too one-dimensional, that we might be missing opportunities. This is a good chance for you to get to know others in the company, share your point of view, and listen to theirs. It will probably be good for you and everyone else."

Brian agreed to give it a try. After a couple of task force meetings, however, he complained to Joe. "These people speak another language. They're talking about identifying and talking with our customers, developing specific products for them, linking with other companies... I don't think they realize where we're coming from. It's going to be hard to educate them."

Joe nodded, amused to hear Brian giving voice to some of the same thoughts he had. "Brian, you're like me. We assume that because we're the old guard, people should agree with us. But it doesn't work that way. Times change. We've got a pretty talented team here. These people are part of the company, and we should take advantage of their ideas. The newcomers give us fresh ideas and challenges. I hope you're listening and trying to understand them." Joe surprised himself at how direct he was with Brian. He hoped he did not come across as too critical.

Brian was not surprised at Joe's comments, though.

"Somehow the past seems so much simpler," he said thoughtfully. "It was just a matter of doing. Now it seems more complicated. I guess we have to keep pace."

"As I've said before, you'll enjoy knowing others in the company. We have a good team here. They certainly will benefit from getting to know you. Let them tell you what's on their minds, you let them know what's on yours, and then go from there. It's give-and-take here, you know."

"I feel like I'm giving up something, but you're right, I know."

Brian worked to listen to others on the task force. He appreciated that Les needed reliable estimates of the product offerings to develop the appropriate marketing staff. Brian was impressed with the arguments of Ron McCarthy from Finance about the great deal of capital needed to bring new products to the marketplace. New products could be great, he said, but they were also great financial risks, especially now that so many companies were interested in electronic medical products. Bill Fredrickson from Production discussed the difficulties and costs of new production. After a time, Brian came to realize that the company needed to become more specific about its strategy of growth through new products.

After two months of work, the strategy task force had circulated its report. Ron, as its chair, gave an overview of the report to the management team. "We had, as they say in diplomacy, a frank exchange of ideas in our task force. But that's not a euphemism for a lack of progress. I think we all learned a great deal and we think our report will be useful to the management team."

Many aspects of the report, Ron began, put down in black and white what is generally widely believed, such as Heart Tech's devotion to improving the health and well-being of its customers through high quality, reliable electronic medical products and to developing the quality of life of its community. Perhaps the most noteworthy and controversial issue was the recommendation that the company form joint ventures with drug companies and others with greater financial assets to develop new products. "Some people wanted to go for the rewards of successful new products, but others were wary of the costs and risks. Joint ventures were proposed as a way to enjoy new products but share the risks."

The task force also saw the need to explore more joint marketing ventures. Marketing agents and agreements with others should be more vigorously pursued. "Overall," Ron said, "we concluded that Heart Tech has too quickly assumed that we should do it all ourselves. We haven't looked for ways we can work with other companies to develop and market our products profitably."

The task force report sparked vigorous, enthusiastic discussion. The consensus was that the task force had identified an important blind-spot in the company's thinking, and that joint ventures deserved serious consideration. After more discussion, the strategy task force was thanked and told that the management team would discuss its report and then meet again with it before drafting a final version.

Management Task Force

The management task force also had its divisions and disagreements. They kept their sights on the developing the best report possible and discussed their conflicts accordingly. Jane Povinsky from Marketing, the chair, introduced the report to the management team. "We took our task seriously and enjoyed its challenges. Indeed, we often had our own task force in mind when we thought about how we want as a company to operate and be managed."

She explained that some task force members wanted a general statement of values and others wanted something more concrete and realistic. After much discussion, they decided that the abstract and specific were both necessary.

They wanted to include the general values that guide how the company is organized, but also include specific procedures that show how the company actually lives these values. The values should inspire the company to develop more effective ways of working together as well as describe the company's present management.

She circulated and discussed the following outline:

I. Employees are valuable individuals.

Value: The individual needs, ideas, and values of employees are respected.

Procedure: People are treated honestly and humanely; deceit and manipulation are not allowed.

Value: Employees are encouraged to develop their skills and to use them for their own and the company's benefit.

Procedure: The company funds and encourages both off and on-the-job training.

Value: Individual rights of self-expression are protected.

Procedure: In team meetings and in other forums, people are given the opportunity to express their views without fear of reprisal or punishment.

Value: All employees are important and must work together.

Procedure: The company recognizes the contributions of all employees through public awards and private appreciation. The company knows that everyone must work together to have a productive organization.

II. Teamwork is vital.

Value: Employees work together to get jobs done; no one person can do the important jobs by him or herself.

Procedure: Employees know they can seek help from others and that they are expected to assist others.

Value: Employees are loyal to their department.

Procedure: They want the best for the whole group and do not just narrowly do their own job or work for their own personal interests.

Value: Managers encourage a team feeling.

Procedure: They consult with group members and ask for their ideas and suggestions.

Value: Problems are approached in a rational way.

Procedure: Individuals do not try to dominate and prove they are right, but use the best ideas to find the right solution for the situation.

Value: Employees aim to discuss their conflicts open-mindedly and constructively.

Procedure: They work to solve issues so that everyone wins, rather than fight to have some win and some lose.

Value: Creativity is valued.

Procedure: People express their ideas, are open to others, and are willing to combine ideas to develop new solutions to problems and foster innovation.

III. The company is one.

Value: All employees recognize that their challenges, job security, and pride depend upon a robust Heart Tech. The company needs to be strong organizationally and healthy financially if people are to feel secure and work productively.

Procedure: The company seeks to share information, responsibility, esteem, and profits among all its employees.

Value: Loyalty to one's group and department should not undercut commitment to the whole company.

Procedure: People realize that it is not just Finance, Production, Marketing, Human Resources, or Research that makes Heart Tech strong, but all of them working together.

Value: All employees have the right and the responsibility to express their views and to contribute to making Heart Tech a company of which they can all feel proud.

Procedure: People from all departments and levels participate on task teams that investigate major issues and propose company policy.

In the discussion that followed Jane's presentation, Barbara observed that these values and procedures would remind everyone of Heart Tech's management and sound ways of working. The team discussed the need to help everyone understand these values and their implications. The task team was thanked and asked to return to discuss a final version.

The next day Brian told Joe that he liked his task force. He felt more aware of the whole company, and enjoyed working with and meeting people from all its departments. "I think you've got something with your teamwork and involvement. I found it amazing that people who think so differently can still work together."

"One thing I've learned is that people have their own perspectives and that most of the time they're valid," Joe said. "At least from their own standpoint, people make sense and have good reasons for their ideas. To work with people and manage them, we must appreciate and use their views, even-perhaps especially—when they are different from our own. When we can get these different people and views going in the same direction and working together, look out! That's when we can really move."

Chapter 11
Making Conflict and the Organization Productive

Conflict revitalized Heart Tech. Through expressing frustrations, Heart Tech people became aware of problems and were motivated to change. By exchanging their opposing views, they created solutions that made them more productive. They were more aware of pitfalls, and more prepared to create new competitive advantages. Conflict kept the people at Heart Tech in touch with each other's thinking and feelings, stimulated ideas, and drove innovation.

But conflict itself did not make Heart Tech effective; its people had to manage conflict. Productively managed conflict was the powerful, constructive force that invigorated, connected, and innovated. Heart Tech people used conflict to control their destiny and create the company they wanted.

Managing Conflict

Heart Tech people, like people in other organizations, discussed many conflicts productively and were able to improve their skills. Managing conflict is within the capabilities of most people. After all, we live with conflict daily, so we have all become skillful to some extent. Unfortunately, we have also developed blind spots and bad habits. People can manage conflicts well, but they need support and guidance. However, many organizations inadvertently make it difficult for people to use their skills to manage their job conflicts.

The ability to manage conflict, though it can be developed, requires much more than knowing a simple procedure or two. Indeed, managing conflict is a complex and demanding process that tests both people and companies. People must be willing and able to express their feelings and ideas accurately, but they must also be open-minded to others, able to develop insights into problems, to create solutions, and persistent in implementing their ideas. Productive conflict requires sensitive give-and-take, creative problem-solving, and gritty determination.

To unlock the potential of constructive conflict, it is extremely important to recognize that there is a better choice than avoiding conflict or fighting to win. People at Heart Tech learned to disagree openly and directly as they worked for mutual benefit. They understood that just because people have opposing ideas and interests does not mean that they need to fight to win or that their goals are incompatible. Indeed, productive conflict is critical if people are to work together as a team and accomplish mutual goals.

Heart Tech people were able to discuss various conflicts cooperatively. Colleagues used conflict to become more self-aware and sensitive to each other. A subordinate handled conflict well to change his boss's attitude from impatience to appreciation. A manager helped two bickering subordinates face their conflict directly. Conflict motivated employees to dig into issues and come up with thoughtful decisions and solutions. Conflict helped Heart Tech managers become aware of the need for a company philosophy and helped them develop one that is realistic.

Making Your Conflicts Productive

It is not enough to say that conflict is a pervasive phenomenon in organizations and that it can't be avoided. Managers must know how to cope with it. People want and need to understand conflict in organizations and to use their conflicts productively. I have not in this book tried to give you a plan for guaranteed success. Conflict is so varied that no one plan is appropriate for all situations. However, the ideas discussed in this book are powerful and can help you develop ways to manage the many kinds of conflicts you face.

You must develop your own concrete plans and steps to deal with your conflicts. But you need not to do this alone. People at Heart Tech turned to colleagues and friends to help them understand the conflict, develop a useful perspective, and decide how to proceed. Most of the people you are in conflict with will also want to handle the conflict well, particularly once it is made clear that there are mutual benefits to be gained. Open relationships and open-minded discussions are invaluable in developing useful strategies. The ideas of this book can help you and your colleagues make wise choices about how to handle conflict. The procedures, strategies, and forums Heart Tech found useful suggests plans you might use to manage your conflicts.

You undoubtedly have already managed many conflicts successfully. You have skills, but you can also get better. Remember, though, that it takes effort, time, practice, and feedback to improve. Learning usually occurs gradually rather than in one giant step. Conflict skills can make you a much more sensitive and effective manager, but you must be willing to work and persist to strengthen your conflict competence.

Cooperative, open discussion is the approach you want to rely on to realize the benefits of conflict. However, it is not appropriate for every conflict. Sometimes you have to fight to win: You initiate legal proceedings against a partner who has exploited your trust. Sometimes you will want to avoid conflict; some conflicts are not worth discussing or cannot be profitably managed. You want to be able to make wise choices about how to handle your conflicts, not be locked into trying to win, avoiding discussion, or working openly for mutual benefit.

Managing Conflict: A Checklist

Managing conflict requires persistence, skill, and ingenuity. At each step in the process, there are several important questions to ask yourself:

Preparation

Are We Creating a Productive Climate for Conflict?

Conflict is inevitable, though potentially constructive. You and your colleagues need to believe you can all talk openly and usefully. People should accept conflict and understand that it can be constructive. The best way to do this is to make sure that your invitations toward openness are not being contradicted by non-verbal organizational messages that people will be punished for speaking their minds.

Have We Formed Strong Personal Links?

Develop relationships characterized by mutual concern and respect. When people feel personally strong and confident, they speak out and deal honestly with issues.

Have We Planned How to Deal with the Conflict?

Conflict requires skilled communication and thoughtful planning. It is not a time to put yourself in "automatic" and let it all hang out. Honestly search to know your true feelings and plan how to discuss the conflict for mutual benefit.

Discussion

Are We Confronting the Problem?

You want to express your views, but at the same time invite others to tell their story. Strive to have everyone communicate ideas, feelings, and hopes in a manner that clarifies the issues and releases tension. People include the facts, goals, interests, and information behind their positions.

Is Everyone Prepared?

Avoid surprises that catch people off guard. Select a time and place so that everyone has the energy, time, and openness to discuss the problem.

Are We Emphasizing Our Cooperative Goals?

Protagonists easily forget their common ground. Define the conflict as a mutual problem for everyone to solve, not a struggle to see who will win. Communicate your intention to work for mutual benefit, and your expectation that others will too.

Are We All Motivated and Empowered?

It takes two to have a conflict and two to untangle. Your wanting to manage the conflict is insufficient. You depend upon others to work on the conflict. Initiate a discussion of the costs to all of the present conflict and how all can benefit from a resolution. Everyone should have the feeling that "We can do it!"

Are We Wary of Our Self-Righteousness?

Especially in conflicts that have escalated, people often feel wronged; the feeling of being right and powerful becomes a self-perpetuating barrier to communication. Self-righteousness, blaming, and finding fault intensify competition. People should recognize how they have contributed to the problem, and focus on working together to manage the conflict, not finding fault.

Are We Walking in Each Other's Shoes?

Conflict is an opportunity to understand another's feelings, views, and thoughts. Show your colleagues that you are trying to understand them by reflecting in your own words their arguments. Then invite others to show they understand your perspective. As a result, you will appreciate the problem fully, understand all sides, and be in a better position to develop solutions that work for all.

Have We Jointly Defined the Problem?

Conflicts defined specifically to everyone's satisfaction are more easily resolved than general principles and grand ideas. Fight over specific issues (the project was not completed on time), not personalities (you are fat and lazy). Stick to the issue and main problem without bringing up tangential issues, taking the discussion too personally, feeling indignant, or trying to save face.

Are We Showing Respect and Acceptance?

Reaffirm the value and competence of others and reduce their fears that they are being rejected as people. Throughout the discussion, avoid challenges and insults that question another's competence and morality. Disagreement is not a challenge to one's value as a person or as a professional that must be defended.

Are We Striving to Reach an Agreement?

Conflict is an opportunity to gather new information and insights and to understand issues more completely. Seek at least compromise measures that lie in between the protagonists' original positions that leave all reasonably satisfied. Better yet, create solutions not previously considered that can leave everyone better off even than their original positions.

Post Discussion

Are We Reaffirming the Agreement?

Show good faith by implementing the agreement. Measure the impact of the solution and discuss ways to make sure it has the desired effects.

Are We Celebrating?

Reflect on the discussion to identify areas to improve, and recognize the courage and skill needed to manage the conflict productively. Celebrate your joint success. Prepare for your next conflict.

Concluding Remarks

Heart Tech people learned to appreciate the positive face of conflict. Believing that conflict is valuable is difficult because prejudices about conflict are strong. Conflict is assumed to be part of the dark side of relationships. We have long been taught that conflict is anti-social and debilitating, that it tears people and companies apart. People, it is said, may take offense and become defensive; they fear their own weaknesses will be exposed, and worry that anger will linger.

Traditional organizational practices have reinforced conflict-negative values. Influential organizational norms enjoin us to be "team players" by not rocking the boat; they equate respect for a person with agreeing with his ideas; they teach that the value of being a "decisive" leader lies in forcing agreement. Because of both this prejudice toward conflict and the difficulty of managing conflict well, it is easy for people to believe they have handled conflict poorly and to wish to be free of conflict.

Heart Tech people understood that conflict pervades social life, but they learned that it is poorly handled conflict that disrupts. Managing conflict, they appreciated, brings rich rewards. They saw that working as a team, like being part of any family, puts them in conflict, and that rather than struggling to create an environment where nobody is willing to "rock the boat," an effective team approach requires open, cooperative conflict.

Conflict is so vital because it energizes people and helps them realize the benefits of cooperative effort. Through working together, people are alert to changes: They develop the confidence to turn problems into opportunities, exchange ideas and information, and combine perspectives to adapt the company and keep it dynamic and innovative. But successful teamwork requires conflict management. No issue is as important for people working together as the ability to make conflict productive. Without this ability, companies and employees stagnate. However, by managing conflict, people overcome obstacles, and meet future challenges.

Reference Note

Many social scientists have contributed to the research upon which this book is based. Morton Deutsch has conducted studies since the 1940's and has summarized his and others' important work in *The Resolution of Conflict: Constructive and Destructive Processes* (Yale University Press: New Haven, CT,1973) and in *Distributive Justice: A Social-Psychological Perspective*, (Yale University Press: New Haven, CT, 1985).

Max H. Bazerman and Roy J. Lewicki's *Negotiating in Organizations* (Sage: Beverly Hills, CA, 1983), Dean Tjosvold and David W. Johnson's *Productive Conflict Management: Perspectives for Organizations* (Irvington: New York, 1983; Now available from Team Media, and Interaction Book Company, 1988), and M. A. Rahim's *Conflict Management: An Interdisciplinary Approach* (Praeger: New York, 1988) are recently edited volumes in which social scientists present a variety of perspectives on conflict in organizations.

Dean Tjosvold's *Working Together to Get Things Done: Managing for Organizational Productivity* (Lexington, MA: Lexington Books, 1986) presents research on conflict and interdependence and its implications for the workplace. Dean Tjosvold's "Implications of controversy research for management" in *Journal of Management*, 11, 19-35, 1985, reviews research on the role of conflict in problem solving and decision making and his "Participation: A close look at its dynamics" in *Journal of Management*, 13, 739-750, 1987, examines the literature showing that positive conflict contributes to successful participative management.

Biographical Sketch: Dean Tjosvold

After graduating from Princeton University, Dean Tjosvold earned his PhD in the social psychology of organizations at the University of Minnesota in 1972, and is now Professor, Faculty of Business Administration, Simon Fraser University, Burnaby, B.C. Before that he taught at Pennsylvania State University and was a visiting scholar at the National University of Singapore. He has published over 100 articles on managing conflict, cooperation and competition, decision-making, power, and other management issues. With David W. Johnson he edited *Productive Conflict Management: Perspectives for Organizations* (Irvington: New York, 1983) and with Mary Tjosvold has written two books for health care professionals.

He authored *Working Together to Get Things Done: Managing for Organizational Productivity* (Lexington Books, 1986), and *Love & Anger: Managing Family Conflict* (Team Media, 1991). He has also recently published *Team Organization: An Enduring Competitive Advantage* (Wiley & Sons, 1991) as part of the Industrial and Organizational Psychology Series and *Conflict-Positive Organization: Stimulate Diversity and Create Unity* (Addison-Wesley, 1991) as part of the Organizational Development Series. Lexington Books will publish his *Leadership: Creating a Team Organization* in 1992. He consults on teamwork, conflict management and related issues in diverse companies and is a partner in several businesses in Minnesota.